M000110616

Danilo, you are a terrific br. for exemplifying a good testimony and being an inspiration for me to serve the Lord with you in Sígueme ministry. I know there were times in your life when things were not easy, but you were always very brave and teachable. Sometimes family and friends failed you, but God's love was your medicine and restoration. In spite of the exhaustion, the pain suffered, rejection, and humiliation, you always had a trusting heart waiting for the Lord's miracle. You are an open letter of God's mercy *and* love, displaying maturity and discipline. In these latter days God has great blessings with the riches, honor, and life that are the reward of the humble and of those who fear God. Remember the words of the psalmist: "Those who sow in tears will reap with songs of joy."

—GUISELLE MONTERO C.
PSALMIST AND COFOUNDER OF SÍGUEME
COSTA RICA

This first book by Danilo will surely enrich the life of many people. In the years that I have known him I have seen a man who is after what's real; that's why all that he shares in this his first book is honest and comes from what God has taught him. I thank my God for my friend and for the motivation that I receive from him.

—JAIME E. MURRELL
ALCANZANDO A LAS NACIONES MINISTRY

Danilo is one of the princes of the praise and worship that God has raised in these latter days to show us His heart. His style of worship is the catalyst that we so need to come before the presence of the Father.

—JESÚS ADRIÁN ROMERO
VÁSTAGO PRODUCCIONES

Danilo, our brother, our assistant (taking care of our children), our student, and above all, our dear friend. We met Danilo when he was just a very confused teenager; we knew him and his struggles and triumphs, but he was always characterized by his search of intimacy with the Father, always wanting to reach the heart of God. Danilo, you had a dream, and your life has been the development and the example of that dream. You have proven that it doesn't matter what our past is. Knowing the love that the heavenly Father has for us, we can forgive all the offenses and not only receive the embrace of the Father, but actually extend our arms to embrace others. We are very proud of you.

—JIMMY AND ILSE COLEMAN
MISSIONARIES
COSTA RICA

When I think about Danilo, I think about a friend, an authentic person, a brother, someone very likable, and above all, a person who knows God. The years have passed, but he remains the same, a Christian with a great servant's heart, a worshiper with the freshness of someone who is always close to his God. What an honor to be able to know the depth of your thoughts in this magnificent book.

—SIXTO PORRAS
EXECUTIVE DIRECTOR, LATIN AMERICA
ENFOQUE A LA FAMILIA (FOCUS ON THE FAMILY)

I have been close to Danilo, from his conversion up until his present ministry, and I could share dozens of anecdotes; but even more than that, I give thanks to the Lord for a sincere, loyal, loving, and worshiping young man who has much to share with all of us who desire to serve the Lord with excellence.

—Pastor Raúl Vargas
Church Oasis de Esperanza
Costa Rica

The day I met Danilo, I embraced him as if God Himself was asking me to use my arms to love him and shelter him. The Holy Spirit said to me, "Adopt him as your son." I couldn't resist it. The experiences in Danilo's life have made him strong and tender at the same time. The main area where he has been molded is in the area of contemplating God's presence. What has made his ministry great and admirable has been the platform from which he ministers: his simplicity and humility. I know that what you will read in this book will enable you to know the true personality of the Father and will encourage you to get closer to Him who suffered so much just because He loved you.

—Pastor Rey Matos
Las Catacumbas Ministry
Puerto Rico

I feel privileged to have met Danilo Montero during his participation in one of the praise and worship conferences that took place in the facilities of Fraternidad Cristiana of Guatemala in 1992. Now it is a pleasure to see how his music, singing, and preaching ministry is known internationally, and I trust God will continue to develop it until it reaches great heights. In this book he now offers us another aspect of his God-given talents.

Let's pray that Danilo's good example inspires many more to walk in the right path and to enjoy *The Father's Embrace.*

—PASTOR JORGE H. LÓPEZ
FRATERNIDAD CRISTIANA OF GUATEMALA

Danilo represents the new generation of emerging leaders whose only commitment is to Jesus Christ, whom they love with all their hearts. His ministry is like a beautiful flower that captivates all those who know him and provokes them to love Jesus. Thank you very much, Danilo, for your life and your example!

—ALBERTO H. MOTTESI
EVANGELIST

Danilo Montero is not only my friend, but even more important he is a friend of God. Danilo's life has touched my heart very deeply. The Lord uses him not only to reach the body of Christ worldwide but also in these days to raise up a generation of ministers who are self-sacrificial and prophetic and who love the presence of the Most High. Finally, a book that has been written that will allow the believer to pursue the embrace of the Father. The principles introduced in these pages will help teach you how to worship, because Danilo, like David, not only knows how to do that, but he also knows the heart of the Father. *The Father's Embrace* is to be read by every Christian who longs for closeness with God and is hungry to know Him. I am very proud of you, Danilo, my friend and my brother in Christ.

—PASTOR SAM HINN
THE GATHERING PLACE
FLORIDA

Throughout my years in the ministry I have seen people of great value who have given their lives in service to the Lord. However, in Danilo I can recognize a man anointed of God to be a mouthpiece and a pioneer of what is true praise and worship as a lifestyle. I can say with confidence that you will enjoy each word in this book as the result of a long walk, where in many occasions, the path has become hard and difficult. Danilo is another witness of the matchless mercy and sweet love of the Father. I know that you will enjoy reading this, because from it wisdom will flow to you and a passion for God's presence that has been mixed with the pen and heart of the writer.

—Pastor Eric Linox
Iglesia Oasis de Esperanza
Costa Rica

THE
FATHER'S
E M B R A C E

THE
FATHER'S
EMBRACE

DANILO MONTERO

Charisma
HOUSE
A Strang Company

Most Strang Communications/Charisma House/ Siloam products are available at special quantity discounts for bulk purchase for sales promotions, premiums, fund-raising, and educational needs. For details, write Strang Communications/Charisma House/Siloam, 600 Rinehart Road, Lake Mary, Florida 32746, or telephone (407) 333-0600.

The Father's Embrace by Danilo Montero
Published by Charisma House
A Strang Company
600 Rinehart Road
Lake Mary, Florida 32746
www.charismahouse.com

This book or parts thereof may not be reproduced in any form, stored in a retrieval system, or transmitted in any form by any means—electronic, mechanical, photocopy, recording, or otherwise—without prior written permission of the publisher, except as provided by United States of America copyright law.

Unless otherwise noted, all Scripture quotations are from the King James Version of the Bible.

Scripture quotations marked NIV are from the Holy Bible, New International Version. Copyright © 1973, 1978, 1984, International Bible Society. Used by permission.

Scripture quotations marked DAKE's are from the Dake's Annotated Reference Bible, copyright © 1996, Dake Publishing, Lawrenceville, GA. Used by permission.

Cover design by Karen Grindley

Copyright © 2005 by Danilo Montero
All rights reserved

Library of Congress Cataloging in Publication Data

Montero, Danilo.
  [Abrazo del Padre. English]
  The Father's embrace / Danilo Montero.
      p. cm.
  Includes bibliographical references and index.
  ISBN 1-59185-549-7 (pbk.)
  1. Spiritual life--Christianity. I. Title.
  BV4501.3.M64713 2005
  248.4--dc22

                            2004016195

This book was previously published as *El abrazo del Padre*
by Casa Creación, copyright © 2001, ISBN 0-88419-715-8.

05 06 07 08 09 — 987654321
Printed in the United States of America

*To the sweet memory of my mother,
Cristy, by whose sacrifices
and prayers I am what I am.*

Heaven must look better with you there.

I will always miss you.

ACKNOWLEDGMENTS

RAÚL, NO ONE has taught me as much over so long a period of time as you have. Thank you for receiving us as a family and for continuing to smile and love us even after twenty-five years, just as you did when we first came to our spiritual house. I want to leave a footprint on others just as you have left in me the simple, yet transcendent, footprint of a pastor.

Jimmy and Ilse Coleman, what did you put in the coffee that so marked my youth? I know what it was: I saw God in you. I saw Him supply when there was nothing on the table; I felt Him listening to me when I needed it, and He counseled me countless times using the love that you profess for His Word.

Rey and Mildred Matos, when the load became heavier, God brought you into my life. I discovered the joy of true friendship and enjoyed like never before the blessing of a spiritual father.

Many thanks to my friend Liz Edén! A little bit of care and a little bit of the "extra mile" have helped me very much to finish this book. My thanks to Tessie Güell de DeVore and everybody at Casa Creación: I would also like to thank the staff at Charisma House for their labor in making the English version of my book become a reality. People who believe in us as you do are like the breeze in the sail of our dreams and who give us the inexplicable joy of navigating to places where we have never been before.

Gisela Sawin, you share my joy of giving "birth" to my first book. Without your editorial help to the Spanish edition, it wouldn't have been possible. I am indebted to you!

George Hernández, Nana, Alessandra, and Rebe, you are the secret heroes behind this book. Thank you for the transcriptions, corrections, and suggestions.

To my friends of Sígueme group and to my ministry team…thank you for believing with me that dreaming is possible. With you my years have become fulfilling, and my calling has become more exciting. We're just getting started on this path!

Acknowledgments

And finally, thanks to you who have prayed for me and for this book. Now that you have it in your hands, it is I who pray that your wait has not been in vain...once again, thank you.

CONTENTS

FOREWORD

Marco Barrientos

THE MEMORY IS very clear in my mind. It was a warm Saturday afternoon in a rehabilitation center for young delinquent girls in Mexico City. Each week, our youth group visited that place to share about God's love, a God who is always ready to forgive and give a new opportunity to those who have failed.

That day, Silvia came to the place where we used to meet, attracted by the music or maybe by the desire to talk to someone because she was bored. Soon it was time to share with her the story of a loving father whose son had returned home after having spent his inheritance living a libertine life—and who received that son with great joy. "In the same way," I said to her, "you have a Father who loves you and is waiting for you to come home."

I wasn't prepared for her reaction. I could see the anger in her eyes. I could feel the hatred in her words when she said to me, "Don't talk to me about a loving father! That's a lie! I hate my father, and I never want to see him again!"

For her, the image of the Father, which should have been synonomous with love, trust, protection, and provision, had been terribly distorted. Once again, the heavenly Father had been badly represented by the cruelty and selfishness of a man who, instead of providing a refuge for his daughter, had sexually abused her and forced her to prostitute herself and to steal from the time she was fifteen.

For a few moments I remained silent, not knowing what to say, helpless before the pain that evidently kept Silvia in a prison of anger and hatred. I remember I could only reassure her that even though her earthly father had abused her, God wanted to adopt her as His daughter, erase her sad past, and take her to the banquet house. When we prayed, I asked God to surround her with His arms of love and to manifest Himself in her life as the Father she needed. Tears quickly filled her eyes, and her hard expression was transformed into a face longing for affection and acceptance.

O, how we need the embrace of the Father! A generation walks and stumbles in their youth, hating their parents and swearing never to be like them, only to inflict the same pain and the same hurts on their own children. O, how we need the safety of a home in which the love, the acceptance, and the forgiveness of the Father create a healthy environment where the most intimate of relationships are experienced, where we learn most of our habits, where we develop our first emotional reactions, and where we make our first decisions about our values.

Only God's embrace is big enough to dissolve our pain with His amazing and unconditional love. Only our heavenly Father is deeply moved by our pressures and problems. Only He can understand us!

That is why I firmly believe that this book, *The Father's Embrace*, will be like fresh water to a heart thirsty for a renewed encounter with the precious grace of our incomparable God. And who better than Danilo Montero to guide us in this healing journey, because everyone who has heard him sharing a message from the Word of God may have noticed that he is an extraordinary storyteller.

Without a doubt, Danilo has distinguished himself as a speaker capable of transporting us with his narrative to the moments in which so many men and women of God lived profound moments of loneliness and confusion, and how the grace of God reached them. At his conferences, the detail with which he describes the encounters that different biblical characters had with God just fascinates me.

But now, in his first book, the author offers us a work that demonstrates that God has chosen him, not only to bring us into His presence in worship and motivate us through his conferences, but also to leave a written testimony of His love. Certainly, not every good speaker is a good writer, but in *The Father's Embrace*, Danilo has impressed me profoundly and has touched my heart.

In the last few years, I have appreciated how God is raising up a generation of young Latin American communicators who are bringing a message of reconciliation, acceptance, and healing to a people devoid of self-esteem and a sense of destiny caused by their spiritual orphanage. My prayer is that this book will be a model of what God wants to do with many other "Danilos" who have been called by God to make a difference in their generation, if they only do as he did and receive the Father's embrace.

—MARCO A. BARRIENTOS
WORSHIP LEADER, AUTHOR, AND FOUNDER
OF "LECHE Y MIEL" PRODUCTIONS
DALLAS, TEXAS

FOREWORD

Marcos Witt

ANILO'S LIFE HAS always inspired me to know God more. Since the first time I had the experience of being in a meeting where he presided over the praise and worship, I was able to attest that he is a man who has a profound longing for God. That longing has inspired literally millions of people to seek the Lord's face even more.

This book comes out of his many experiences, both in the ministry and personal. It is a beautiful story about the need to know God instead of knowing *about* God. We have a great need to pause and recognize that many times we speak of God without really knowing His heart.

As I read this manuscript, what impacted me more than anything is the openness with which Danilo speaks to us. As a reader, I could tell he was speaking to me from his daily experience, not from some theoretical dream. With great tact he leads us through a series of very intimate thoughts and experiences that have led him to question much of his actions and activities. The question I heard throughout the whole book is this: "Do you know God religiously or personally?" Honestly, this question touched my heart. It is when we ask ourselves this question frequently that we will be careful to not incur religiosity, and we all know that the last thing we need in America is more religion.

I am certain that as you read this book, you will find yourself more in love with the Lord. When I came to the last chapter, I found myself with teary eyes as I thought how beautiful my Lord is and how much I really love Him.

Thank you, Danilo, for making me love my Lord even more, not only with your life and your songs, but now also with this—the first of many books with which God has blessed your hands.

—MARCOS WITT
PASTOR, WORSHIP LEADER, AUTHOR,
AND FOUNDER OF "CANZION" PRODUCTIONS
HOUSTON, TEXAS

FOREWORD

Pastor Sam Hinn

A S A FATHER, there is no greater joy on earth than when I can love on my children. I love expressing my feelings to my children—hugging them, kissing them, telling them how much I love them. My love for them is not contingent upon whether they reciprocate my love or not; I love them unconditionally. But they know they melt my heart when they do show me love.

I remember one early morning when our daughter, Christa, came into our bedroom waiting for us to wake up to give us a big "good morning" kiss. As soon as she saw that we were half-awake, she gave Erica and me a big kiss and jumped into bed to snuggle with us. A few minutes later, she was asking for breakfast. So much for that! But we enjoyed every second of her doting her love on us.

Tenderness. Love. Warmth. These are words that pop into my mind when I think of a father's embrace. But to know the love of my heavenly Father leaves me longing for more of Him.

In 2000 I made a trip to Costa Rica with my friend Danilo, where we had the privilege of ministering to hundreds of worship leaders, singers, and musicians. God's presence was so powerful during that conference that many of those worship leaders flooded the altar, longing to know Him more. On the night before this outpouring, July 5, the Lord gave me this word:

> These are the days of longing. I am going to bring you into a place of longing for Me. I will become that all-surpassing gift in your life. I will bring you into the exceeding, abundant life of My Spirit. These are days of longing, either a longing for Me or a longing for things that do not pertain to Me. I am longing for you. Are you longing for Me as I am longing for you?...I am raising up a people of longing in these days. A people ruined for ordinary living, people of longing. I am looking for a people of longing.

I stayed up until the early morning hours that night, seeking His face and searching the scriptures that confirmed this word. Since that time I have seen this prophetic word come to fruition. There is a stirring, a longing, for the Father's embrace in these last days as never before.

Danilo Montero is my brother in Christ, but he is also my friend. I know him as a renowned worship leader who ministers to thousands and yet remains humble and pliable to the Spirit's leading in his life. He is a man who knows firsthand how much our heavenly Father longs to reach out and embrace us in our present condition. As you read, you will see how it was Father God's gentle touch that comforted a frightened little boy during a turbulent moment. It was Father God's irresistible tenderness that wooed Danilo when he ran away from His presence. It was the unconditional love and warmth of the Father's embrace that captured Danilo's soul and where he still remains today.

This is the Danilo that I know. This is the man who is about to guide you on your journey back to your Father's presence. There is no formula, no religious rite, or no tradition that will get you there. Get ready to open your heart, mind, and spirit and drink in the presence of your Father, for whom you have been searching. These are the days of longing. He is longing for you. Are you longing for His embrace?

—Pastor Sam Hinn
The Gathering Place

MY SOUL THIRSTS FOR GOD, FOR THE LIVING
GOD. . . . DEEP CALLS TO DEEP.

—PSALM 42:2, 7, NIV

INTRODUCTION

WHEN I WAS in my twenties, it was a habit of mine to buy *Life* magazine, because I enjoyed the pictures. One of the images I will never forget is that of two newborn twins. The article told of the amazing story about their difficult and premature birth. One of them came out of the incubator just a few days after being born, but the other newborn had to remain. Despite the doctors' enormous attempts, the newborn's condition was critical, even to the point that they began to fear they would lose him. One of the nurses who took care of the sick baby and who had grown fond of him had an idea: she brought his little brother and laid the newborn beside him. To her surprise,

1

almost immediately, the healthy boy reached out his arm and wrapped it around his sick brother. The picture showed them lying facedown, to the left, the little one, small and weak, with tubes coming out of him, and to his side, hugging him, was his brother. The scene is moving, but even more amazing is what happened later. A few hours later, the newborn began to eat the food he seemed to reject earlier, and little by little, the medicines proved effective. The medical staff was able to witness a true miracle—the miracle produced by the bond between two brothers.

We human beings long for a connection that we lost in the past and that we define through pictures kept in our memories: the smile of a loved one who has left us...our father's lap...the long hours of playing in the country with our brothers and sisters...the smell of the house where we grew up...the smell of our first schoolbook...the warmth of the womb that sustained us. We don't miss those moments as much as we miss the people who made those moments memorable. We long to feel connected with others, loving them and being loved. That is, in essence, the home that our souls search for.

Many of us build a "house" with sand and cement where our souls may build that "home" together with our loved ones. For others, that home is found in the heart of a companion or in the sweet company of our brothers and friends.

The home that we yearn for—beyond sepia-colored photo memories—is the home we left because of disobedience, a garden we lost, and, in it, a true Father—the one who gave us life.

That spiritual connection is the beginning of all our dreams, the very reason for our existential longing. We miss His tender voice, His wise counsel, the warmth of His gaze, and the solace of His embrace. God the Father is the fountain from which we spring and to which we desire to return. His love is the fountain of all love and the substance of all that can satisfy the human soul. In His love, He

To be able to admit that we long for that connection with our Father is the starting place of true spirituality.

created us and gave us a name, and encompassed in that name is our true identity and the sublime purpose of our existence.

Some go through life denying this spiritual desire; others prefer to calm the restlessness of the soul by trying to drink from the finite fountains of human love. Others rush to build broken stairs to reach toward heaven, or they weave a glamorous dress that will protect them from the cold of their needy soul with the fleeting warmth of religion.

No matter what path we choose to follow, our spirits will

continue to shout: "Where is my Father and my God?"

That is the voice in anguish of the fallen race incarnated in the dying Son.

> My God, my God, why hast thou forsaken me?
> —MATTHEW 27:46

At the crucifixion, the Son of God, taking our place, said the prayer existent in the spirit of man, the plea of a child for his Father; such plea finds an answer only in the surrender of our spirits in the hands of God:

> Father, into thy hands I commend my spirit.
> —LUKE 23:46

To be able to admit that we long for that connection with our Father is the starting place of true spirituality. Genuine fellowship with God is the theme of this book. I trust that as you read its pages, you also will travel through the pages of your soul and renew your hunger for God. The road at first may seem rough, for you may have to admit that you left stumbling blocks hindering your path that need to be removed. It is a road that requires of you to be honest enough to admit that you have hidden behind fears, pride, and religiosity, doing anything you could to avoid a face-to-face encounter with your Father. However, this encounter that you so fear is the ultimate goal of your spirit and is the mountain where your soul sees God and finds rest again. Discover those hidden obstacles in the fugitive heart of Jonah, in the arrogant spiritual robe of the Pharisee, or in Jacob's elaborate deceptions. Maybe you will see your face in theirs, as I found mine. If you do, each one of them will invite you to follow only one path. Some were pushed by waves; others found a way amidst judgmental looks; others, like Moses, crossed mountains that shook and passed clouds of fear; but all were able to arrive.

Follow their example! They blazed a new path not difficult to reach. In fact, it starts with only one step, with a prayer, and with a determination: "I will return home." Onward then! Uncover the veil, climb the mountain, turn the page. On the other side the Father's embrace awaits you.

No one is more a slave than he who lives at the mercy of his own selfishness, and no one is more free than he who has surrendered his will to another one when that other one is God.

Chapter One

In the Belly of a Fish

M Y PASTORS HAD decided to send the whole pastoral team to receive biblical training in the United States. Because of this, Raúl, one of the pastors, asked me to be his assistant. At that time, I was seventeen years old and had recently finished high school. I gladly accepted, hoping that the experience would help me confirm God's calling to a ministry. I had actively served in my church for more than five years as a deacon, youth president, and a teacher in the children's ministry. However, that new responsibility prompted me to attempt to double up on my spiritual practices. This was very hard because I had placed on myself the burden of the self-imposed expectation of being an example and fulfilling what I thought everybody wanted me to be as a leader.

During that time, I would pray four to five hours a day. But my prayers were long, solitary monologues. They were five hours of "perfect" intercession, but not of sweet fellowship with God. I would fast at least three times a week. My life was dominated by compulsion to perform.

I doubled my efforts to be an exemplary Christian, but the more I tried to reach spiritual goals, the stronger my human nature emerged. That was how areas of my life began to surface that I had never dealt with adequately, in particular those doors open to sin.

When my pastor confronted me about these things, he discovered in me a stubborn and rebellious person. This situation caused a strong confrontation between us, and, finally, I felt accused of things that I thought I hadn't done. Then, I simply exploded and left the church.

I went to college and started a new stage: a process of deliverance on the one hand and of enslavement on the other. I freed myself of the masks that were unconsciously hiding my true emotional countenance. That was good and brought healing, because it gave me the opportunity of knowing and accepting myself. But, because I was so immature in the handling of my new "freedom," I abused it and opened my soul to everything that would take me further away from God.

An Uncomfortable Surprise

As I attempted to travel new "paths" of disobedience, I found myself surprised by a startling discovery: the further away I wanted to go, the closer I perceived God's presence. I had a notion of His presence accompanying me wherever I went. I am not speaking of a mental, religious "programming" that somehow conditioned me. I am talking about a genuine "experience" with His presence. God became an unexpected companion, a "spoilsport" who ruined some of my rebellious adventures; at least that's how I perceived it for some time. His presence became so uncomfortable that I simply couldn't sin with pleasure.

How was it possible that He would be with me when I wasn't seeking Him? The same presence that, in anguish, I had sought as a teenager was now unavoidable. Sooner or later, I had to admit that God was not just an "idea" enclosed in the church system; He was a reality I had to deal with somehow.

There were two factors that influenced me to return to God: First, my friends, the Colemans, and second, an encounter with God.

Jimmy and Ilse came back to God as a result of the financial and marital crisis they faced after a life away from the faith. Their house was a refuge to me in my youth, especially when things would get difficult at home.

Behind closed doors I would find the normal dynamics of any family: work, ironing clothes, changing diapers, paintbrushes, and furniture to be made. However, the daily routine was frequently interrupted by Ilse singing praises and playing a tambourine while her four children, dancing expressively, followed her around the house. The Word of God was the usual subject, and prayer was like the long-awaited "dessert" after a good talk.

How was it possible that He would be with me when I wasn't seeking Him?

The Coleman's contagious passion touched me during that crisis. I wanted the faith that connected their hearts to heaven and yet kept their feet firmly grounded here on earth. There were no religious stereotypes or rigorous demands; it was a genuine experience with God.

Second, I had a transforming encounter with God. It was a holiday weekend, and I had made plans with my friends. But while planning what I would do, again I felt God's presence walking by my side. I got angry and argued with the Lord for a while, and I said to Him, "I am tired of You seeking me out.

You spoil everything. Why don't You stay in the church, or if You want to, in my room? Leave me alone. I dedicated my life to the church, to Your service, and as far as I can see, I haven't gotten anything in return. In the church I was treated unjustly. That's why I want nothing to do with You or with the church. If you are looking for me so that I may serve You, You can give up now. I will never serve You again."

Then I recognized God's voice speaking to me: "I want you to know that even if you never serve Me again, I will continue to love you the same. I don't love you for what you do for Me but for who you are. You are My son, and there's nothing you can do to change that."

Hearing His voice changed my rebellion, and He brought me back to His love.

It was then I discovered how sinful and rebellious I could be as a human being, but I also saw what we usually don't realize: how much the Lord loves us.

Nothing conquers the hard and rebellious soil of the human heart as does the "banner" of His love revealed to us. That tireless love pursues us and attracts us with cords of forgiveness, melting down the ice of resentment, warming us up against His chest. There is no hardness that can resist the sweet touch that humbles and seduces us.

In my youth, I wanted to surrender my heart to God based on harsh disciplines, restrictions, and much service, but I was unsuccessful. Now that I had nothing to offer; I was loved as intensely as ever, only now I knew it!

After that encounter I felt an intense spiritual hunger. Before that experience I wanted to "do" a lot of things, because I was pursuing a ministry that I thought would please God. Now I was following the Lord, and my only desire was to know Him more intimately. I dedicated the next few years to seeking God in prayer, worship, and meditating on His Word.

CONFRONTING OUR SECRET

The story of Jonah is that of one who, like me, wanted to flee God's presence. The Lord had asked him to go to Nineveh, Assyria's most important city. According to information that we obtain later from the prophet Nahum, Nineveh had committed sins such as thinking bad things against God, exploiting the destitute, cruelty in war, worshiping idols, prostitution, and sorcery. This city was approximately five hundred miles northeast of Israel. Jonah had to warn them of the imminent punishment and declare to them that they could obtain mercy and forgiveness if they repented.

Jonah wasn't just anybody; he was a man anointed of God. Perhaps he had already accomplished other important missions. The task of evangelizing the capital of the world was a job only for a hero of the Spirit, the type of person who knows God and is trained in the hard battles of the Spirit.

God had reviewed that list several times. No one in the whole kingdom qualified for this task as Jonah did. The problem is that Jonah did not want to go.

Wait a moment, Lord, Jonah thought to himself. *I know You. You will forgive them after I preach, and I don't want that to happen. I hope that city, the capital of sin, will be judged. That kingdom of uncircumcised men must pay for what they have done to Your people.*

Could it be that this was the reason why Jonah resisted going? We don't know the truth with certainty. This supposed internal monologue only tries to illustrate what could come out of this hero of God's heart. Ultimately, the

> *Why do some ministries retreat just at the door of the pinnacle of their calling? What is the reason we face the most decisive test when we are the closest to our dreams?*

one most surprised about this reaction wasn't God, because He already knew it, but it was Jonah himself.

When the prophet asked, "And where is Nineveh supposed to be?" God's finger pointed toward the east. Immediately, Jonah got up and ran exactly in the opposite direction; he escaped to the west. He bought a one-way ticket and boarded the first ship he found to go as far away as he could.

His destiny was Tarshish, known at that time as the end of the earth.

How could he do such a thing? Especially if we take into account that he was about to receive a supernatural "promotion" in his ministry. In a few days, thousands and thousands of people would come to the kingdom of God as a result of his preaching. A kingdom would be forgiven, a city saved from judgment, and the name of God made known. Everything that a servant of God dreams of accomplishing some day was just around the corner for Jonah. His prayers would be answered, and his desire to be used would be fulfilled.

Why are there times when a human being does exactly the last thing he should be doing? Why do some ministries retreat just at the door of the pinnacle of their calling? What is the reason we face the most decisive test when we are the closest to our dreams?

This is due to the fact that before we can see higher places in our spiritual experience, we must cross the narrow bridge of confrontation. The divine door to new dimensions of anointing and service is obedience.

The truth is that before touching the fresh green of a new spiritual field, God will cause us to discover the only thing that can hinder our relationship with Him, the hidden secret of our heart: our rebellion.

Rebellion? In a servant like Jonah? In me?

A PUSH OF GRACE

But a strange storm broke out above the escape ship. Soon, the tanned skin of the runaway felt the cold impact of the drops of rain, and the strong breeze announced a change of plans.

In the meantime, each one said to his companion, "Come, and let us cast lots, that we may know for whose cause this evil is upon us" (Jon. 1:7). When they did that, the lot fell on Jonah. And as the sea became more and more rough, they asked him, "What should we do with you?"

Jonah said "Take me up, and cast me forth into the sea; so shall the sea be calm unto you: for I know that for my sake this great tempest is upon you" (v. 12).

A few minutes later, the sailors were holding Jonah by his hands and feet, and, at the count of three, he was thrown into the sea.

The storm calmed. The dark clouds disappeared, the wind ceased, and the waves died off. In an instant, the sun reigned in the firmament, and the seagulls took up their dancing flight in the Mediterranean sky again.

There are times when our disobedience deserves a push from God.

Bob Fitts told us a funny story during a praise conference. When he was a professor of the School of Worship at the University of the Nations in Hawaii, he organized a day trip for the students. The river entertained the group for many hours, and the day seemed perfect until something happened. A student looked toward the waterfall that was behind them and, shouting, invited the group to climb up and then jump from the top. His colleagues did so immediately, all except Bob.

"Look, Bob, this is incredible," they said while jumping off. No one could discern what was behind the teacher's nervous smile, so they insisted that he jump. The pressure from the group was stronger than his fear, and Bob accepted the invitation.

He was able to reach the edge of the waterfall, only to greet all his students as they were signaling from below for him to join them. It was at that moment that his paralyzing fear forced Bob to turn around and return to the security of the edge. Then came "the push." Without knowing how, his foot slipped on a rock, he lost his balance, and his head hit the bottom of the river. Once he overcame the whirlpool of bubbles and regained consciousness, his friends clapped amid smiles of the accomplishment. Bob, in the meantime, greeted them raising his fist like a champion celebrating his victory.

Sometimes the "pushes" from God are circumstances that seem to change the course of things and that make us lose control. However, they are excuses that He uses to "push" us toward His heart. Just like the baby who is forced out of the womb by the laws of nature to the strange outside world, we also cry, ignoring the fact that this is the path, the only one, to become a complete man or woman.

Those waves that Jonah experienced followed the rhythm of God's heartbeat. The winds carried His voice: "Return, My son!" In the meantime, Jonah went away swimming westward.

In the Prison of the Heart

The Lord had prepared a great fish to swallow Jonah. God was determined not to play a game of cat-and-mouse with Jonah for too long, so God decided to corner him. It was then that the fish's huge mouth opened up and began to swallow hundreds of gallons of water into its dark inner part. It was there that the obstinate one ended up. The fish was God's answer to Jonah's escape plan.

How would he get out of there, if escape were even possible? The uncertainty and oblivion played with the fetid smell of seaweed and dead fish. Jonah was trapped in the belly of the fish for three days. He had never felt so alone, so far from the world, from the light, and from his destiny. He descended to the lowest point, to the place where there are no friends, and prayers don't seem to work.

If anyone felt mistreated by life and by circumstances, it would be Jonah. If anyone could bemoan the weight of the problems, it was him. If anyone could think himself far from God, it was Jonah.

19

What would you have done in his place? Many of us quit attending church; others blame God for the strange things that have happened to us. We argue, "How can I follow You, Lord, under such difficult circumstances?"

Often we, God's children, find a reason within the circumstances to not have a profound friendship with Him. "My job is terrible." "The environment in my neighborhood doesn't allow me." "If you lived in my house, you would know why it is so difficult to have fellowship with God."

These, and others, are our excuses to try to avoid having a love commitment to God. Your grumpy boss, your unbelieving husband, or your rebellious son or daughter is not the problem. And neither is the enslaving routine of home and children. It is not your family or your culture. Such things would seem to be prisons, but the wall that exists between your heavenly Father and you is not made out of place, time, and space.

> *Do you feel cornered by a specific situation? Are you asking the Lord why the limitations? Are you praying, "Lord, get me out of here! Where are You? Why don't You change things?"*

Do you feel cornered by a specific situation? Are you asking the Lord why the limitations? Are you praying, "Lord, get me out of here! Where are You? Why don't You change things?" Then you are in the same situation that Jonah and I had to go through: the bridge of confrontation.

> Then Jonah prayed unto the LORD his God out of the fish's belly, and said, I cried by reason of mine afflic-tion unto the LORD, and he heard me; out of the belly of hell cried I, and thou heardest my voice. For thou hadst cast me into the deep, in the midst of the seas; and the floods compassed me about: all thy billows and thy waves passed over me. Then I said, I am cast out of thy sight; yet I will look again toward thy holy temple. The waters compassed me about, even to the soul: the depth closed me round about, the weeds were wrapped about my head. I went down to the bottoms of the mountains; the earth with her bars was about me for ever: yet hast thou brought up my life from corrup-tion, O LORD my God.
>
> —JONAH 2:1–6

Jonah prayed to the Lord his God from the belly of the fish. The fury of the storm, being a castaway, the raging waters, and the decomposed algae did not stop this moment. Jonah turned to God. This prayer is a testimony, a song to the faith-fulness of God and a liberating confession.

This scene represents the prison of the human heart, our self-sufficiency. Jonah was trapped in the belly of the fish until he finally recognized that he was, in reality, enclosed in his own sin. It was in the brokenness of his pride where he found freedom. Jonah didn't ask to be taken out of there; he only confessed his sin, because what imprisoned him wasn't animal skin but a rebellious heart. There is no greater slavery than being at the mercy of one's own selfishness. There is no greater liberty than surrendering one's own will into the hands of God. When Jonah realized that his ideas were vain, he renounced trusting in his flesh, and he repented.

Human beings need confrontation to discover what is in their heart. Once their secret is discovered, they have the option of becoming hardened or broken; if they choose the latter, they find the freedom of the soul.

The prophet offers himself to God once again, and in his prayer of consecration he affirms, "I will pay that that I have vowed" (Jon. 2:9).

What does the prophet promise? He promises to say what God tells him to say, to do what He asks him to do, and to *go wherever he is sent.*

It is there, in that place of consecration, that the person finds God and finds peace. When chapter 2 of the Book of Jonah begins, the story is repeated as if the first chapter did not exist. Except that this time Jonah runs in the right direction...he follows God's finger.

A SECOND CHANCE

After all that adventure, Jonah discovered a God who grants new opportunities. He recognized that it is not the places or the people who surround us who hinder us from experiencing God, but it is our own attitudes. When pride, vanity, and unbelief are confessed, then comes that experience. Jonah discovered a presence that is not limited by storms, whales, or even rebellion. The presence of God pursues us until it conquers us.

Similar to Jonah, I discovered that the presence of God is greater than the circumstances of life. I also learned that the human heart is the only wall that darkens the light of His presence. I was also able to understand that for the hardness of the soul, God has the remedy, and it is brokenness. When we are willing to admit our mistakes, the warm presence of the Father reveals itself again to us in grace.

Do you want to live more intensely in God's presence? Then don't refuse being confronted with the truth. Do you long to climb to a higher dimension? You must cross the

Do you want to live more intensely in God's presence? Then don't refuse being confronted with the truth.

narrow bridge that causes the heart to surrender. Are you complaining about a "prison" from which you want to get out? Why do you not listen to His tender voice pointing toward the secret of your heart?

Are you running away to Tarshish? Are you crying because you do not perceive God? Have you not heard Him? He is screaming in the waves and whistling in the wind. His eye follows you, and His soul misses you.

Don't be amazed if on the way His love surprises you.

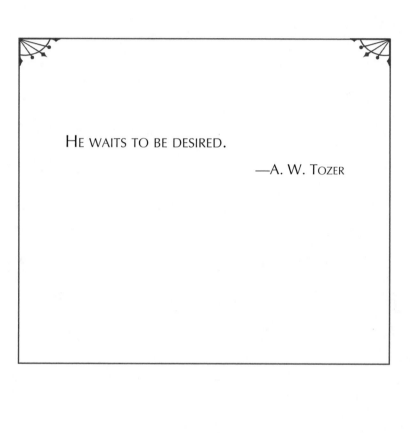

HE WAITS TO BE DESIRED.

—A. W. TOZER

CHAPTER TWO

RAIDERS OF THE LOST ARK

URING MY ADOLESCENT years, I used to attend the annual national youth camp in my native country of Costa Rica. Over one thousand kids full of enthusiasm would come from different cities to a remote little town in south Costa Rica called San Luis de Buenos Aires. It was a time of genuinely searching to receive more of God.

If we didn't arrive early—and we almost never did—we ended up sleeping in "the henhouse," a wooden structure with a metal roof where you could use someone else's stinky feet as a pillow.

There we slept, a few dozen kids, in large bunk beds. It was extremely hot, the mosquitoes were insatiable, the beds hard as a rock, the serving lines at mealtimes were long like a summer without water, and the restrooms—or better yet, the latrines—indescribable. The only attraction was the river. Swimming in the river there was quite an experience.

But in spite of all that, the spiritual blessing was fabulous. We would spend entire nights in vigil. The meetings were saturated with the Word and visitations from God. I can say, without a doubt, that those were some of the best moments of my Christian walk.

The ride back home was superb. The bus was filled with nonstop praise, prayers, laughter, and tears. When we would stop to eat at some restaurants along the way, there were people who would convert to the Lord. We were overflowing with God's presence!

But the euphoria wouldn't last long. A few weeks later we would be facing the same indifference as before in the meetings. What was wrong? Why did it seem to be so difficult to maintain our spiritual experiences? Why was it so easy for us to get out of His presence?

A VISITATION FROM HEAVEN

Today it is a challenge for me to face large audiences with thousands of young people waiting to be ministered to. At each meeting the burden to help this generation discover a relationship with God resurfaces. More than I want them to have a beautiful experience at a concert, my desire is to see young people establish a steadfast relationship with God. I want them to understand that a friendship with God is within reach.

But there are enemies in their hearts that desire to interfere in that relationship with Him, and one of them is religiosity.

Our relationship with God is based upon what He already did to reach mankind. But religion is what mankind does in their anguish to recover what was lost in the Garden of Eden.

In order to worship the true God, we need to know Him. But we can only know Him as He reveals Himself to us.

In every human being exists the tendency to pursue spirituality—an innate religiosity, that is, that part of me that wants to please God. Such "intuition" led us to create images of the deity that conform to our necessities instead of seeking the revelation of the true God. Moved by that "need," we human beings have created systems of worship that would serve us as steps to ascend to His presence. In other words, our human race has become a victim of the "Babel syndrome," when we have believed, in arrogance, that we could elevate ourselves to God's heights by our own means. Assuming that, we have ignored a fundamental principle: *In order to worship the true God, we need to know Him. But we can only know Him as He reveals Himself to us.*

That is why it is imperative that we comprehend the essence of the gospel, because only in the gospel is the face of God revealed to us clearly and faithfully. At the same time, it is the good news that offers us the path to true "spirituality;" a relationship between God and man where God provides the initiative and the means, but man responds through faith, surrender, and obedience. In the gospel we are portrayed as religious and the substitutes that we have loved more than the "truth" of God are exposed, and we are invited to draw near to Him.

We must confront our religiosity when we discover it. It is the first adversary that chases away God's presence. I want to invite you to travel back in time to a wonderful story, which is found in the first Book of Samuel. It is the story of a religious woman and the miracle of her encounter with God. It is the account of an anointed child and the spiritual awakening that he brought.

THE BARREN ONE CONCEIVES

Now there was a certain man of Ramathaim-zophim, of mount Ephraim, and his name was Elkanah, the son of Jeroham, the son of Elihu, the son of Tohu, the son of Zuph, an Ephrathite: And he had two wives; the name of the one was Hannah, and the name of the other Peninnah: and Peninnah had children, but Hannah had no children. And this man went up out of his city yearly to worship and to sacrifice unto the LORD of hosts in Shiloh. . . . And when the time was that Elkanah offered, he gave to Peninnah his wife, and to all her sons and her daughters, portions: But unto Hannah he gave a worthy portion; for he loved Hannah: but the LORD had shut up her womb. And her adversary also provoked her sore, for to make her fret, because the LORD had shut up her womb.

—1 SAMUEL 1:1–6

Hannah had everything a woman could wish for in life. She was beautiful. She was the kind of woman that had a circle of admirers among her neighbors. Furthermore, she had a husband who loved her more than anything and a "good religion." Every year, their faith and good financial position took them to the place of worship in Shiloh to offer abundant sacrifices to God. They were good people!

Elkanah made sure that Hannah felt special by telling her, "You are the best thing ever to cross my path. Hannah, with you I'm fulfilled. Children? You don't need to have them for me to love you. Besides, I already have them with Peninnah."

When the message entered Hannah's ears, her expression, which had slightly relaxed, became rigid again.

Elkanah constantly tried to fix the situation: "Hannah, you are better to me than anything else. Sweetheart, you have me.

Or am I not man enough to make you happy?"

Hannah had her husband, she had her religion, and she had a good life, but she didn't have children (1 Sam. 1:2).

That year, her husband took her again to Shiloh. Somehow, the trip was good for her. Almost always her beloved's countenance improved after being in the house of God.

The ceremony began. Two young priests would call upon the name of the Lord, and then the pilgrims would bring one by one their offerings—birds, lambs, cakes, and calves. The weariness of the trip had not diminshed the intensity of the devotion that accompanied each sacrifice. A worshiper would cry in silence while putting his hands upon the small animal, and the priest would cut its throat with the knife. Somewhere else a child, leaning on his father's shoulders, was listening intently to the explanation of the rite—abundant smoke, blood on the floor, smell of incense, and clean consciences.

Hannah also brought her animal. Her long, black eyelashes soaked up a small tear. After it was done, Elkanah looked at her with a nervous smile. Hannah avoided his look. They didn't talk on their way home.

"That was a good meeting, right?" asked her upbeat husband.

"Yes, it was," answered Hannah half-heartedly.

The meal on the table was left almost untouched.

Peninnah's children were playing with the food while she tried to control them. Peninnah returned from the kitchen with dessert. She kissed Elkanah, and while she leaned on his shoulder, she looked at her children. Before sitting down, she cast a conniving look at Hannah.

Hannah got up from the table, put a shawl over her head, and opened the door.

Startled, Elkanah asked her, "Where are you going?"

"To the Lord's tent," answered Hannah.

"But Hannah, the service is already over. There is no… Hannah, wait."

The door closed. The only thing Elkanah was able to hear was the sound of the sob muffled by the clothing. The curtain was opened, and Hannah's beautiful silhouette was projected against the tent's thick curtain. You could still notice the strange smell of the ashes and the incense of the sacrifices. Hannah went in, guided by the flickering light of the menorah, and leaned against one of the poles that held up the tent.

She tried to pray. She said a few old prayers she had learned from her father. She wished the priest was close to help her offer her sacrifice again. It would be easier if a schedule guided her in this awkward moment. She felt uncomfortable because she had always come with something in her hands, but now they were empty.

"I have nothing to say. I don't want to! Lord, Adonai," was all she said, and she sank back into her silence—the long silence of her life. The silence of fear, of the routine—of religion.

What do you do in moments like these? What is appropriate to sing or to say?

Every minute is an hour, and each heartbeat is a year.

You don't speak to avoid offending. You don't dare articulate words because they haven't taught you. You want to be right. Your fear is that your sincerity may be used against you. You don't want to hear the superficial answers or the rebukes that others have given you before: "Have faith." "You did something bad." "You're not praying enough."

Also, you don't communicate because you don't know the heart of the One listening. You remain silent because you have been there many times, acting, following what others do. But you never knew the One who was there, seeking you in every song. You were never able to see the One calling you behind every testimony. You couldn't read the message behind the message. The silence has been a curtain that hasn't allowed you to see the One behind all this. You can't see the One who lovingly calls you from the other side.

And neither do you want Him to see what is on this side of the silence—your heart. It has been easier to wear the familiar cloak of habit.

The routine of religion leaves us sterile. That is why every Sunday, Latin America is filled with millions of worshipers in the churches. Prayers are recited and sermons are preached, but people leave without having crossed the line of religion—the line that separates tradition from an encounter with God. For the majority, it is OK that things remain the same, because our own customs have taught us to go to "God's house" without really expecting to meet Him there.

The rite must be fulfilled, the program must continue, and our tradition must be perpetuated. There is no contact, interaction, or intimacy. We are afraid of being in the place where we won't know what to do in the exasperating wait of the one who wants to hear or see God.

That is why we leave unchanged week after week, month after month, year after year.

> And as he did so year by year...
>
> —1 SAMUEL 1:7

Is it possible that Hannah went to "worship" God every year without experiencing any change? Yes, it is possible to go unchanged, because religion leaves its followers sterile and voids the power of God in the believers. At least, it is so until we decide to cross that line. And that is what Hannah wanted to do.

And she was in bitterness of soul, and prayed unto the Lord.

—1 Samuel 1:10

This time, as the sun was setting, the cloak of pretension was rent from the soul of the barren one. And as a river that overflows with all its strength from the rocky prison that held it back, her tears came down.

Hannah cried about Peninnah's schemes, the beauty of children not her own, and the fear of being cast aside. She lamented the lost years, the arms that never held anyone. She cried about the emptiness left by religion.

> *The ability to bare the soul is what takes us to the point of change.*

Her cry opened a space in her soul for faith. The search prepared her spirit for a new revelation from God. In her anguish, she touched God, and in her touch, grace overflowed.

Grace? By the way...that is the meaning of the name *Hannah*. The grace that makes possible the impossible, that touches us when we find His presence.

Those features marked by the sadness in Hannah's face

were transformed by joyful gestures:

> So the woman went her way, and did eat, and her coun-
> tenance was no more sad.
>
> —1 SAMUEL 1:18

Once you discover the presence of God, you are never the same. That's what happened with Hannah, because the answer to her request changed her life. God granted her the desire of her heart, and she had a boy whom she named *Samuel*, which means "asked of God." Another suggested meaning of the name is "God has ears."

Religiosity breaks down when the worshipers discover that their God listens! The moment that God's name stops being passively frozen in the pages of tradition is when we start a new path. From that day on, Hannah worshiped a living God, not just an idea.

Heaven waits for people who dare to cry before God. There is a pressing urgency for transparency in those who come near to worship. The ability to bare the soul is what takes us to the point of change in which the church will find itself at the dawn of a new day and will give birth to a generation with prophetic character, a people who know their God.

Not only was Samuel the answer to a woman's need, but he also became the spearhead of a new move of God among His people, a move that confronted Israel's religiosity.

There are four characteristics of religiosity that are exposed in the story of Samuel and Eli's sons.

1. Lack of knowledge of God

In those days the judges still ruled Israel. Eli was judge and high priest of that nation. His sons were also priests of the house of God, in the city of Shiloh. They held the most important position of service in Israel's worship. However, the public recognition only helped hide the terrible way in which they handled their private matters.

> Now the sons of Eli were sons of Belial; they knew not the LORD.
>
> —1 SAMUEL 2:12

These two men were raised in the house of God; they knew the tabernacle's operating manuals like the back of their hand, and they were worship experts. But when God has to testify regarding His ministers on earth, we hear something like, "They don't know Me, and they have nothing righteous within them."

Is it possible that there are priests in the house of God who do not know Him?

Eli's sons had been educated with the high priest but had no spiritual life. They had a religion, but they didn't have a relationship. They had the customs but not the experience. Those who had been chosen and anointed with holy oil suffered from spiritual ignorance.

Eli's sons are the example of a generation that was born in the church but who has never been born again. They are the prototype of a generation that loves their denomination but don't live in devotion to God. That generation lives in Hannah's barrenness because they practice the rites but do not enjoy "life" in God.

2. Insensitivity to His presence

When each Israelite offered sacrifices to God with holy fear, the priests were present at the offering. They would send their servants to stand next to the Israelite who was offering sacrifices. While the meat was roasting and they asked forgiveness for their sins, the servants would take the best part of the meat and would leave. Before the meat was presented in sacrifice, as the Law commanded, they would almost snatch it away from the hand of the person offering it. Furthermore, they would eat it before the fat burned, which violated God's law according to the Book of Leviticus. (See 2 Samuel 2:13–16).

According to the Law, all the needs of the Levites had to be met through the tithes of the people. But Eli's sons would take advantage of their position to satisfy their own desires. The disregard and arrogance they manifested toward the people and the worship eroded the integrity of the entire priesthood. So great was these priests' ignorance that they had lost all fear of God. The altar had no value to them, and because of their sins, the people themselves began to disregard God's worship.

> The sin of the young men was very great before the
> LORD: for men abhorred the offering of the LORD.
> —1 SAMUEL 2:17

The lack of respect for God's presence is another characteristic of religiosity. Is praise provoking the emotions of the people, or is it the altar where we present our offerings in holy fear and adoration? How many times do we look at our program first rather than what God wants to do? How often do we "stop" the flow of the Holy Spirit in worship? Aren't we perhaps despising the Lord's offerings when we limit the move of the Holy Spirit in the middle of a service?

If there is a flippant attitude in our hearts before His presence, God demands repentance, because the true sin behind this is ignorance.

In Israel's temple there were priests, but they were not people who spoke on behalf of God. They were busy with their religious things, but they didn't guide the people to God's presence. They had expertise in the religious rites, but they couldn't help the Israelites to discern the will of God in their lives.

> And the word of the LORD was precious in those days;
> there was no open vision.
> —1 SAMUEL 3:1

If there is something that the Holy Spirit desires in these days, it is that we wake up and recognize our heart's condition regarding His presence.

There are two reasons why this spiritual "sensitivity" is essential. The first reason is that true holiness comes from it. When we are sensitive to the Holy Spirit, we respond quickly when He lets us know that we have grieved Him. Knowing how to respond to the directions of the Spirit is what keeps us in this purity and makes us mature.

The second reason is that our constant response to His presence leads us to a life of friendship with God. Cultivating God's presence is the spiritual exercise that takes us to a deep relationship with Him. In fact, the principle is applicable to us who lead others in worship to God. I can say, without a doubt, that the difference between the one who leads the singing and the one who guides others in worshiping God lies in the spiritual sensitivity.

In the last ten years Latin America has experienced a spiritual awakening of great impact. The continent was renewed in areas like music, liturgy, and church growth, among other things. The praise and worship move brought a new spiritual song, and with it a fresh perspective in approaching the Lord. One of the greatest accomplishments of this move is that it made us reconsider the importance of God's presence in our lives and meetings. Did we get the message? Or are we only going to enjoy the music?

With the renewal of praise, some put away the old organ and fired the old missionary lady who had played faithfully for the last twenty-five years. Others went so far as to hold a "burning" of hymnals to celebrate the farewell to the old tradition. It pains me to think that such interpretations of God's move were so wrong.

> *Knowing how to respond to the directions of the Spirit is what keeps us in this purity and makes us mature.*

Many churches made room for a set of drums, guitars, a bass guitar, and a praise team. In this new openness, the youth took responsibility for the music in their churches. They have done their best to bring the people up to date with the latest praise hit on the Christian station's "heavenly hit parade." And all of that has been very positive.

I still remember my first visit to Santiago, Chile over ten years ago. I ministered along with my brother-in-law, Rodrigo, for two weeks in a small church outside the city. The people responded with enthusiasm to the songs and the Word. Several weeks after, I received a letter from a lady whose words encouraged me and made such an impact: "Your songs put words to the cry for God that is in our hearts. After so many years singing the same songs, those new songs came like a drop of water in the desert."

Latin America needed that renewal. The current generation needs new ways to express their hunger for God. The gyms, temples, and stadiums became too small to hold so many youth who gathered to sing, pray, and seek God. We live in a special and exciting time!

But I wonder if we really understand the message behind the music. Have we learned to love God's presence? Are we a people ready for His presence? Are we, as Vivien Hibbert defines it in her book *Prophetic Worship*, "students" of His presence?

3. Moral corruption

> Now Eli was very old, and heard all that his sons did unto all Israel; and how they lay with the women that assembled at the door of the tabernacle of the congregation.
>
> —1 SAMUEL 2:22

Hophni and Phinehas, the sons of Eli, had defied all respect to the point of sleeping with the women who served at the entrance of the house of God. The lives of these priests stunk just like the religiosity we pretend to keep as proof of our Christianity. Religion hides filth underneath its robes.

This is why religious pride makes us err. It makes us believe we are better than others because we don't do certain things and because we do our Christian "duties." We ignore that the only thing that makes the life of a Christian wonderful is God's presence. If we ignore that presence, we put out that flame, we bury that holy altar, and we become submerged in sin's filth.

Moses understood how essential God's presence was among His people. They had just heard the sad news that God would not guide them to the Promised Land because of Israel's sin. Instead, an angel was promised to them.

> Leave this place, you and the people you brought up out of Egypt.... I will send an angel before you... But I will not go with you.
>
> —EXODUS 33:1–3, NIV

In this circumstance, Moses prays one of the most dramatic prayers recorded in Scripture. In his intercession, the leader of the nation responds to the Lord:

> You have been telling me, "Lead these people," but you have not let me know whom you will send with me.... If your Presence does not go with us, do not send us up from here. How will anyone know that you are pleased with me and with your people unless you go with us?
>
> —EXODUS 33:12, 15–16, NIV

44

4. Lack of spiritual victory

Neither Eli's sons nor the people knew how far they were from their faith until they had a battle.

> Now the Israelites went out to fight against the Philistines. The Israelites camped at Ebenezer, and the Philistines at Aphek. The Philistines deployed their forces to meet Israel, and as the battle spread, Israel was defeated.
>
> —1 Samuel 4:1–2, NIV

In their distressing defeat, the Israelites went to God. At least that's what they thought, because they sent for the ark of the covenant. The ark was the most sacred artifact in the worship to God (v. 3).

They took the ark of the covenant to the camp. This encouraged the Israelites, who received it with great joy. But nothing could stop the fatal outcome: neither the ark, nor Israel's shouts of praise, nor the fear of the Philistines. Thousands died, including Eli's two sons, and even more so, the ark was stolen (vv. 4–11).

The ark no longer represented the holiness of God's presence among them. A symbol of God does not guarantee His presence and power. It was a generation that didn't have victory. The Philistines defeated them because they were not spiritually victorious. The Bible defines this group as "a generation without glory."

When the news reached Eli, who had already lost his sight, physically and spiritually, he fell backwards and died.

Hearing such calamity, Phinehas's wife gave birth prematurely and in her dying moments named her son with a revealing name, *Ichabod*, which means "without glory." She never knew that in naming her son that name, she had unveiled the name of a nation without God, a generation without victory before the enemy, a people without His presence.

FINDING THE LOST ARK

Thank God the story doesn't end there. The Lord already had a plan of restoration. God had His sights set on Samuel.

What a difference between the ways of Eli's sons and young Samuel's ways! While Eli's sons despised God's presence, Samuel ministered to the Lord, dressed in a fine linen ephod brought to him every year by Hannah, his mother (1 Sam. 2:18).

The ephod was a long, sleeveless vest used by the priests. Samuel was dressed like a priest even though he wasn't one. While Eli's sons despised the Lord's offerings, Samuel was learning to minister with holiness even in the smallest tasks in the temple. While they had a public ministry, Samuel simply cleaned up the blood from the sacrifices, swept the ashes, put oil in the lamps, and dusted the utensils before God.

When they slept with strange women, Samuel rested…near the ark of God (1 Sam. 3:3).

So God looked for Samuel in the night. While Eli slept the mortal sleep of conformism, and while his sons sinned near the altar, God looked again for someone who would still be interested in Him.

He looked for someone, before Israel would be lost in the night of her forgetfulness, before there was no remedy:

> The lamp of God had not yet gone out.
> —1 SAMUEL 3:3, NIV

And God found him asleep in His presence.

That child had taken his mattress and placed it near the ark. What was he looking for there? What did he think about before going to sleep? Maybe he said to himself, *Where is the God of this ark? What happened to the glory that shown on it? What happened to the light that would scare away Israel's enemies and would make His children tremble in reverence?*

Is it because no one seeks You anymore? Why do You not speak? Why do You not talk to me? I want to know You! I want to seek You! I will come again and again until something happens. If everybody else stops coming, I will stay here until You appear. I will remain here every night, waiting…even if I fall asleep.

And then it happened…

> Then the LORD called Samuel. Samuel answered "Here
> I am."
>
> —1 SAMUEL 3:4, NIV

Hannah's child found the God of his mother. And God found a vessel, a new stock of priests, a new generation.

Samuel is a symbol of an extraordinary generation, a generation thirsty for God and that does not stop until they find him. They are a people who leave their religiosity to find what religion has lost: the glory of His presence!

The Bible doesn't say who was the next high priest. In fact, it couldn't have been Samuel because he was not a direct descendent of Aaron, but he acted as high priest at that time, offering important sacrifices for all Israel. Samuel was the last judge in Israel and the first priest and prophet that served during the time of a king.

> *Lord, we pray asking Your forgiveness for our frivolous attitude in Your presence. Make us faithful priests who live in Your presence. Make us priests who serve You and know You. Raise up from this generation an army of priests after Your own heart.*

AS LONG AS WE TRY TO BE THE CAUSE OF THE SUPERNATURAL, WE WOULD REMAIN IMMERSED IN RELIGION.

—ARTHUR BURT

CHAPTER THREE

THE CROSSROADS OF CHANGE

WHEN I WAS a student in grade school, the teacher would make us form a single line according to height before entering the classroom. I hated being the first one in line. By fifth grade, we (boys) began to notice that the girls were growing much faster than we were. That was quite uncomfortable. That concern grew when my friends began growing also. I couldn't deal with this dilemma any longer, so one day I asked my parents during lunch, "Why does everybody grow and I don't?"

I can still remember my family trying not to laugh. My mom, being wise and compassionate, said to me, "Honey, don't worry about it. Some people begin to develop very early, and after they reach a certain height they stop growing. But others grow little by little. And there are still others who seem to remain small, but then suddenly, in their adolescence, go through a growth spurt...and, well, they catch up with the other ones."

Those who know me would know, before I mention it, that I am still waiting for that growth spurt.

Growth was also a very important theme for me in my adolescent years. Only now that I knew Jesus, the question had a more profound implication: How can I grow spiritually? How can I break this spiritual lethargy and maintain growth?

The answer implies a truth told in the parable of the Pharisee and the tax collector. It is found in Luke 18:9–14.

This short story answers a crucial question for the Christian: can anyone come into the presence of the almighty God and leave in the same condition?

> Two men went up to the temple to pray, one a Pharisee and the other a tax collector. The Pharisee stood up and prayed, "God, I thank you that I am not like other men—robbers, evildoers, adulterers—or even like this tax collector. I fast twice a week and give a tenth of all I get."
>
> —LUKE 18:10, NIV

That was his prayer.

The tax collector, however, with a different attitude, came before God beating his chest, and with his eyes looking to the ground, he said, "God, have mercy on me, a sinner."

Jesus finished His parable by saying, "I tell you that this man, rather than the other, went home justified before God. For everyone who exalts himself will be humbled, and he who humbles himself will be exalted" (v. 14, NIV).

THE PHARISAIC SYNDROME

The Pharisees were a group of religious men dedicated to teaching. They promoted the development of the religion in the synagogue. They were truly committed to training the people in the knowledge and practice of the Law of Moses. Several Pharisees accepted Jesus, and many of them were baptized. The most famous among them was Saul of Tarsus.

In their eagerness to teach the Law, they fell into the error of using it as a means of self-exaltation and, at the same time, as a controlling tool. In the end, what was once a deep passion was transformed into an unhealthy religiosity. This group became one of the bitter enemies of Jesus and was involved in the conspiracy to judge and kill the Savior.

Jesus was relentless with them and used them as examples to warn us of the errors that nest in the human heart and keep it from a genuine spirituality.

Seeking a Connection

Jesus described the Pharisee's posture before God as "standing," which demonstrates his self-confidence, and we can deduce his prayer was based on his religious "performance": "I fast twice a week."

In the mind of a Pharisee, God was the guardian of the Holy Book. To please Him, one had to follow His law to the letter. Performance was first, and the relationship with God came as a result.

For the Pharisees, their love for God was measured in terms of personal religious accomplishments. This is the kind of person who longs to be loved by God and bases the degree of God's love on his potential to "accumulate" points with God. It stands to reason that the person seeks to minimize his mistakes as much as possible, because they are synonymous with God's rejection. On the other hand, doing what is "right" is equated with being loved and accepted. Consequently, divine love can only be "secured" through perfect achievement.

At one point in my youth, that was my supreme goal. My service to God was my cry for His acceptance. For this reason my service became obsessive—teaching children, leading the youth, preaching, helping in the television ministry, cleaning the classroom, counseling someone, evangelizing. All of this was due to a need for love. I tried to be "the good guy" in my school, always reading my Bible and watching my conduct and testimony. I wanted to be an example to my friends in the church and to impress my leaders and God.

Where did this need come from? Perhaps it stemmed from my search for paternal acceptance in my childhood. Dad had been a good man. He had provided very well for our needs, but he didn't have the ability to communicate love. In a family of five children it was bound to be difficult to have the opportunity to establish a real contact with him. And even though I longed for it, I never knew how to find that bond.

I knew what Dad liked. He loved soccer. As the benefactor of a soccer team, his business was always full of soccer players and hosting championships.

> *Anyone who follows the path of the Pharisee will live in the ups and downs of a faith based upon personal accomplishments.*

I tried to learn about it, but I didn't get past the first class. Of course, I didn't finish well. Deep down, I didn't like soccer.

I tried to convince him to take me to the stadium, as he did with my older brothers. One night he promised to take me, but in a moment of distraction, my dad left with my brothers. I ran out the door and went as fast as I could toward his business. When I got to the corner, the taxi had already left. As I watched it drive away, I also gave up any hope of having that emotional connection. My dad was physically present but emotionally absent. Finally, when I was around ten, Dad left home.

A person who, like the Pharisee, seeks that kind of connection with God is not capable of finding it. His image of God is so distorted that it causes a terrible insecurity in his faith. Anyone who follows the path of the Pharisee will live in the ups and downs of a faith based upon personal accomplishments. Therefore, he will have to come to grips with the reality of not being able to "reach" God through his "flawless" conduct.

PRIDE: BUILDING ON SINKING SAND

The person who acts like a Pharisee is incapable of praying because he doesn't know how to have intimacy; he doesn't understand that spiritual connection. But rather, he compares himself to everybody else and falls into the error of finding himself to be the better person with a self-adulatory comment: "I thank You that I am not like other men."

His focus, then, is on himself instead of God, because in light of his own judgment, the Pharisee believes he is worthy of exaltation because he has an advantage over others. This is the wrong focus based upon the wrong foundation: his pride.

The Pharisee's pride went before him. That's why as long

as we are immersed in the pride of thinking we can do it by our own means, we will be immersed in religion, and therefore, we will not change.

The apostle James takes an X-ray of the spiritual condition of the church in his letter:

> What causes fights and quarrels among you? Don't they come from your desires that battle within you? You want something but don't get it. You kill and covet, but you cannot have what you want. You quarrel and fight. You do not have, because you do not ask God. When you ask, you do not receive, because you ask with wrong motives, that you may spend what you get on your pleasures.
>
> —JAMES 4:1–3, NIV

Many people struggle to change, but they can't. They struggle trying to be the best, to reach a high spiritual stature. They desire the anointing and victory others have, but they don't obtain it because they do not ask. They don't have the ability to pray and articulate their needs.

And why is it that we do not ask? Because the one who is prideful does not know how to ask and does not desire to ask, much less to receive!

On the one hand, pride inhibits us to ask, and on the other hand, it ties our hands to receive what is offered to us.

"When you ask, you do not receive…" in reality carries

the idea of asking and not being able to receive.

The same passage teaches us:

> But he gives us more grace. That is why Scripture says: "God opposes the proud but gives grace to the humble."
>
> —JAMES 4:6, NIV

When you study this passage carefully, you discover the connection between the first and the sixth verse. Behind the wars, fights, divisions, coveting, envy, and inner conflict is pride.

All of these are the wrong ways that we choose to express our frustration for wanting to change but not knowing how. And we don't know how because we don't depend on God in prayer. That's why He cannot pour out His transforming grace on us, because our pride has covered our eyes and tied our hands.

God gives grace to the humble. And who is humble but he who knows how to ask? Besides, asking is appropriate of a son or daughter. In the act of asking we show trust and humility. Prayer and humility are intricately woven.

In my rebellion, I grew up convinced I shouldn't ask anything of anyone. I forced myself to save so that I wouldn't have to ask my dad for money. As a teenager I got a scholarship so that I wouldn't have to depend on anyone, and while I was in college, I worked to pay for my studies. My financial independence was only an indication of my personal pride.

When the Father revealed His love to me, it broke my self-rule and pride.

Pride has infiltrated us so deeply that we do not recognize it. Many years ago I heard someone say that pride is like bad breath; everybody has it but you.

Pride not only takes away our capacity to pray or ask, but it also pushes us to compare ourselves with others. Many nations suffer from the syndrome of comparison, the same syndrome as the Pharisee. My country has prejudice against the country next to it; the other one thinks it's better than us. We confuse patriotism with pride. We base our lives on comparisons. "Because I have better things, I'm better than my neighbor." "I have a better education than someone else, so I am better than him." "My last name is European and yours is native." We are always comparing how better we are than everybody else. Each church council says, "We have the complete gospel; the others do not. We speak in tongues; the others do not. We dance in the Spirit; they don't do it."

We seek to base our lives upon false pretenses that make us feel prideful. Even the Christian system functions that way; we exalt the charisma, fame, and popularity of people.

Someone is more important if he or she visited several countries, has more degrees, or wrote more books. They are all references to success and popularity, and it is not that these things in themselves are bad; it is what we do with them that causes damage.

How does God treat pride in us? He uncovers it, confronts it, and breaks us. In fact, the only remedy given for the haughty spirit is, "*Humble* yourselves..." (1 Pet. 5:6, emphasis added).

RELIGION: A FALSE HOPE FOR CHANGE

The pharisaic attitude manifests itself in the exaggerated emphasis of the form: the strict fulfillment of the norms, the length of the hair or of the dress, and white shirt or the tie. While we meticulously observe these things, we forget the brotherly love, the unity of the church, honesty, and mercy.

Jesus denounced the Pharisees for giving primary importance to what was secondary and vice versa:

> Woe to you, teachers of the law and Pharisees, you hypocrites! You give a tenth of your spices—mint, dill and cummin. But you have neglected the more important matters of the law—justice, mercy and faithfulness.
> —MATTHEW 23:23, NIV

To a Pharisee, the most important thing was the external appearance. But in emphasizing this, we see the chaos of religion, because in the search for a perfect image, the search for a pure, internal life is neglected.

> You clean the outside of the cup and dish, but inside
> they are full of greed and self-indulgence.... You are
> like whitewashed tombs, which look beautiful on the
> outside but on the inside are full of dead men's bones
> and everything unclean. In the same way, on the out-
> side you appear to people as righteous but on the inside
> you are full of hypocrisy and wickedness.
>
> —MATTHEW 23:25, 27–28, NIV

The Pharisee wants himself to be the cause of the supernatural: purity, holiness, and justice. Everything that only
God can do, the Pharisee pretends to obtain by his own
means.

God is not a perfectionist; He *is* perfect. Perfectionism
seeks to obtain an excellence of character or of discipline
in order to exalt itself above others or to impose itself upon
others. It seeks to control other people through its supposed example. We must be an example, but not with the
goal of enslaving others. This way of thinking seeks to control people through the fear of not pleasing God and fear of
punishment if certain disciplines are not fulfilled.

In my youthful vanity I was able to reach a spiritual position
that made me feel satisfied. I was an example to others, the
youngest preacher of the congregation and the most spiritual
young man in the whole area.

I prayed for two hours faithfully and eagerly read the Bible. I
fasted so much that on some occasions my mom would ask me

nervously in the morning, "Are you going to eat breakfast?"

"No, I'm going to fast again!" I responded.

And then my mom, worried, would say, "But, son, in order for a spirit to fast, it needs a body." (In case you didn't get it, there's a joke in those words: I was so skinny that I almost didn't have a body…Forget it!)

I tried to dress like a preacher to show that I was a committed Christian. Many other young people tried to reach this same goal by a strict spiritual discipline through fasting, long prayer times, and piling up biblical knowledge.

Why is this emphasis wrong?

Because it assumes that spiritual change comes from the external things we do.

Paul warns us that even though the external disciplines have a certain value, they cannot, in any way, give us victory against the appetites of flesh.

We all have a Pharisee within us. It is a child seeking a bond with his father, a good man who ignores that this goodness is not enough. A daring adolescent who wants to climb a ladder to heaven without anyone's help, whose determination blinds him so that he doesn't see that his ladder is broken.

THE OTHER CHARACTER: AN UNWORTHY SEEKER

This personality is the collector of taxes and customs. At some point in history this title was an honorable one, but then these men were hated by the people, excommunicated from the synagogue, and excluded from normal dealings. Consequently, they were forced to seek the company of people who led easy lives, "sinners." Their tendency to charge more than what was required and their exclusion from the religious society are reflected in different parts of the Bible. For example, read the story of Zacchaeus, "a chief tax collector," and Matthew.

The tax collector was a despised person. Considered a traitor within the Jewish community, he served the Roman Empire by collecting taxes for them. Tax collectors pressured the Jewish people and stole the taxes from them to give to the nation's enemy.

> But the tax collector stood at a distance. He would not even look up to heaven.
> —LUKE 18:13, NIV

The tax collector bows down before God and doesn't even dare look up. This is the physical expression of a heart attitude—to bow down before God and to acknowledge who He is. His heart was broken. His brokenness of heart and humility captured God's attention. He then asks the Lord to change him: "God, have mercy on me." He had the right approach!

This man's prayer contains an honest definition of himself: I am a sinner. But at the same time, he doesn't focus on himself, but rather he reaches out to God as the focus of his spiritual hunger. For the person who knows his condition, it is easier to receive the good news when heard. The Pharisee had to be convinced of his condition because he considered that he didn't need help. The tax collector knew he was a sinner and that he had no worth before the people. Consequently, he sought God, and that attitude opened the door to divine grace.

> ...me, a sinner...
> —LUKE 18:13, NIV

Finally, when this man defines himself as a sinner, he offers us an honest description of ourselves. Brennan Manning says this: "What we deny cannot be healed."[1]

If you don't identify your sickness, you cannot seek the medicine.

THE PHARISEE'S LIFE VS. THE TAX COLLECTOR'S LIFE

The Pharisee talked to himself and about himself, but the tax collector prayed to God and was heard. The Pharisee could see the sins of others but not his own. The tax collector, on the other hand, focused on his needs and candidly admitted them.

The Pharisee boasted; the tax collector cried. The Pharisee returned home worse than before; the tax collector went home forgiven.

The lesson and warning in this story was for the Pharisee. Humility is the mother of all virtues, just as pride is the father of sin. In the case of man, humility is having the capacity to recognize who each one is: we are sinners, a race that fell and that made the wrong decision. But, at the same time, we can recognize who God is: "My Creator, my God, my answer, my solution, my life, the source of everything good that could happen to me."

I started this chapter with a question: how can I grow spiritually? And the answer implies a truth, which is told in the parable of the Pharisee and the tax collector. This short story answers a crucial question for the Christian: can a person enter into the presence of the almighty God and leave the same way he came?

The tax collector teaches us that the door to the Father's presence and heart is humility, which is defined as the key to a spiritual change. Pride, which is the greatest obstacle, prevents us, therefore, from coming closer to God and believing in Him.

Do you want to grow spiritually? What will you do when you find yourself at the crossroads of change? One sign points to the south: to your home, your pride, the Pharisee within the heart, the masks, and the substitutes.

The other sign points to the north: to your God. It is the path to the humility of the heart, sincerity, and dependence.

GRACE IS RECEIVING WHAT WE DON'T DESERVE. MERCY IS NOT RECEIVING WHAT WE DO DESERVE.

—UNKNOWN

CHAPTER FOUR

GRACE IS AN EMBRACE

G IVE ME!" WHEN those words were spoken at the table that morning, the father closed his eyes in pain. He looked for that spark of love he had seen in his son's eyes, but he didn't find it. Instead, there was a frown on his face and a demanding, elusive, distracted look.

That was the same look that the young man had the day before when the father tried to find out what was wrong with him. For a week now, he had noticed him waking up late to go to work, his chores were incomplete, and his seat was empty at dinnertime.

The father had considered reducing his work, which went from morning to sunset. He wanted to discuss it during one of their usual nightly walks that they so much enjoyed, only his son chose to be in his room and listen to his music.

While he thought about the possible reason, he remembered finding him looking through the window with his gaze fixed toward the west. What does the west have to do with this change? Trying to fit the pieces of the puzzle together, he also remembered that afternoon when his son stopped to talk to some foreigners. They looked quite young, and the conversation went very long amid laughter and jokes.

Finally they left, and his son waved good-bye to them as if he were waving good-bye to old friends. For the next hour, his son remained leaning against the fence that led toward the road, his face in his hands, as if he were daydreaming, mesmerized by the lights in the distant west.

He couldn't understand what was going on. He had given him all the love he could possibly express. Because this son was the youngest, he was able to dedicate more time to him than to his older son. He was the pride of his old age. He had seen him grow and become a strong young man, decided and loving.

"Dad, did you hear me?" asked the son, quite upset.

"I'm sorry, son," he answered quickly. "I don't understand. Why do you want the inheritance now? Do you need something? You know that you can have whatever you ask for.

Everything in this farm is yours; you know that, right?" the father continued.

"It isn't that, Dad. It's just that I am so tired of cows and pigs. Before, I loved everything, but now I have lost that love. I feel like I am dying here among the hay, rakes, and buckets. I need a change...I want my life! My own life!"

"Son, you have your life secured here with us," replied the father while he tried to hug him.

"Let go, Dad. I'm not a child! Can't you see? I am suffocating here! I'm going to die if I have to stay here beside you while there is so much to see out there!

"Haven't you heard, Dad?" he continued his argument. "There are cities on the other side of the mountain where the lights never go out and friends are always plenty. I am bored with these wooden walls, dinner always at the same time, my brother's criticism, your orders, and my clumsy work. I want my part, I want my life...I have a right to."

"Son, this breaks my heart. However, I don't think you care about that. I'll give you what you ask. Only answer this before you go: When did you stop loving this house of fellowship? How did the delight of serving me become a nuisance to you? Who has stolen your attention and hindered our friendship? Since when has your soul been absent at our table? What window has seduced your senses? What has become more important than our encounter?

"What was the strange fire that was more captivating than the warmth of my presence? Tell me if you know. Answer me if you've realized it.

"When did I ask you for a sacrifice instead of devotion? Did I ask you for service instead of passion?

"How long have you lived in my house but have been looking outside through a window? How have you deceived yourself?"

The old gate creaked. The father looked through the window while his son drove away, leaving behind a cloud of dust that stretched into the horizon. The house was silent; all that was heard was a sob, and from the outside, the workers remember seeing a shadow, the motionless silhouette of the father praying, almost glued there by the window that looked toward the west until night came.

Lights are flickering, and the streets are packed. You can hear the sound of footsteps running back and forth.

"Sale"…"Welcome"…"Try it now"…the clanging sound of coins can be heard and the ring of the machines. "Summer Fashions"…"Happy Hour"…laughter and beeps announcing it is midnight. In the dance clubs…revealing clothing, body language, people who talk with just a look. It is Friday night.

Daylight dawns and Sunday rolls around once again.

Ten messages on the answering machine, twenty calls to make, credit card payments, the empty wallet...

THE FARAWAY PROVINCE

Why spend money on what is not bread, and your labor on what does not satisfy?

—ISAIAH 55:2, NIV

After he had spent everything, there was a severe famine in that whole country, and he began to be in need.

—LUKE 15:14, NIV

The province of desire is also the place of spiritual disgust. There is such emptiness behind all its lights and pleasures. It drains your strength, but you do not see the fruit. You spend your resources, but nothing brings happiness to your soul.

Though you do a lot, you don't get anywhere. You have become unfruitful.

The singing doesn't move you; the preaching bores you. All you have are yesterday's experiences. Nothing satiates you; nothing satisfies. Neither the friends from church, because you do not want to see them, nor the friends from the outside, because they disappeared. Nothing entertains you; everything bores you. There isn't a program that pleases you.

You ask yourself why you feel this way, even when you attend church.

You have noticed that even though you visit the Father's house, you still live in a "faraway province."

You suffer from spiritual anemia, and you don't even know it. You have become like the believers in Ephesus:

> I know your deeds, your hard work and your perseverance.... You have persevered and have endured hardships for my name, and have not grown weary. Yet I hold this against you: You have forsaken your first love.
>
> —REVELATION 2:2–4, NIV

You have lived through the silent process of your deteriorating faith. It is during this time when you suffer the symptoms, but you are not always aware of the cause.

This "faraway province" is a place where you serve obsessively, but you do not find rest. You lack strength to pray, lack faith to ask, and don't even have the desire to sing.

> So he went and hired himself out to a citizen of that country, who sent him to his fields to feed pigs. He longed to fill his stomach with the pods that the pigs were eating, but no one gave him anything.
>
> —LUKE 15:15–16, NIV

This "faraway province" is a condition of the heart that leads us to further degradation. The person who wanted to escape from the work at the farm ended up working on a farm. This time he was forced to do so. Even to the point of craving the slop that the pigs ate.

The story of the prodigal son is our story also. It's the tale of many preachers' kids who left their parents' home to waste their spiritual resources. It is the X-ray of the religious heart that, even though it is physically present in the "house," its soul has been seduced by the distant "lights."

The path of the prodigal is that of the church's lukewarm heart, an inner path through which we have descended, almost without noticing. When we wake up from our spiritual astonishment, we find ourselves eating the leftovers, but we do not know how we got there. It didn't happen overnight; it was a slow process, sometimes taking years.

When young King Hezekiah ascended the throne, he began a process of spiritual renewal. When he called the leaders to repentance, he let them know how they had come to the state of spiritual sickness in which they were in.

> For our fathers have trespassed, and done that which was evil in the eyes of the LORD our God, and *have forsaken him, and have turned away their faces from the habitation of the LORD, and turned their backs. Also they have shut up the doors of the porch, and put out the lamps, and have not burned incense* nor offered burnt offerings in the holy place unto the God of Israel.
> —2 CHRONICLES 29:6–7, EMPHASIS ADDED

As you can see, spiritual decay is a slow process that takes us from a meaningless lack of interest to open rebellion.

But how do we get out of there? Fortunately, the story doesn't end there. In the next few verses, three principles of restoration are described for the heart of a "prodigal son."

1. Discover your real spiritual condition

> When he came to his senses...
>
> —LUKE 15:17, NIV

When this happens, it's as if suddenly the scales fall from your eyes. Someone who is passionate for God makes you feel like an ice cube. Maybe a simple song or a word will make you wake up from your dream.

When I came back to the Lord at age nineteen, someone gave me a cassette from the late pianist and singer Keith Green. The name of the cassette was *No Compromise*. His words penetrated my lukewarm soul like a lightning bolt of confrontation and exhortation. His prophetic voice made me cry and shake before God.

Many years later, I had the privilege of experiencing something similar when I heard famous Spaniard Christian artist Marcos Vidal's album *Seek Me and You Shall Live*. When I heard the first lines of that song, I almost fell to the ground crying and asking the Lord to revive my life again.

> Remember the height from which you have fallen! Repent...
>
> —REVELATION 2:5, NIV

The worst sickness you can have is the one you don't recognize. That was the Laodicean church's disgrace. They believed they were OK, but their spiritual condition was very grave.

> You say, "I am rich; I have acquired wealth and do not need a thing." But you do not realize that you are wretched, pitiful, poor, blind and naked.
>
> —REVELATION 3:17, NIV

Before coming back to the Father's house, it is necessary that we recognize where we really are and repent. Repentance is not a one-time event, isolated in the life of a Christian. It is a *lifestyle*. We need to learn to live with it. This is a door to return to the Father.

2. Desire to change and confession

> I will set out and go back to my father...
>
> —LUKE 15:18, NIV

There is an anguish in the soul that pushes us toward heaven. It's the spiritual hunger that awakens in the person who returns to God. The spiritual desire is a sign of a divine visitation. We need to desire more of God, desire more of a profound change, and cry for something fresh once again.

This desire to change is manifested in the sincere confession:

> ...and say to him: Father, I have sinned against heaven and against you.
> —LUKE 15:18, NIV

> *We need to desire more of God, desire more of a profound change, and cry for something fresh once again.*

For spiritual change to take place, confession is indispensable. Remember how useless the Pharisee's prayer was because he was incapable of recognizing his spiritual bankruptcy? In contrast, the tax collector's confession earned God's transforming grace. It is necessary that we call sin for what it is: sin. As long as we attribute our failures to others, we continue to walk in spiritual darkness. In the next chapter, we will take a closer look at the place confession has in our lives.

3. Decision

> So he got up and went to his father...
> —LUKE 15:20, NIV

We can cry about our failures forever, but nothing will change unless we decide to follow a new course. We can forever dream how we would like to be, but we won't reach our God-given destiny until we "get up" from where we are today.

We have to make decisions. Sometimes we will have to make a decision about a relationship, changing jobs, giving up something, or going back to the simplicity of our initial search.

> Remember the height from which you have fallen! Repent and do the things you did at first.
> —REVELATION 2:5, NIV

RETURNING HOME

> But while he was still a long way off, his father saw him and was filled with compassion for him; he ran to his son, threw his arms around him and kissed him.
> —LUKE 15:20, NIV

Another day was ending at the farm. The animals had just been taken back to their pens. The house was filled with the delicious smell of supper being prepared by the servants. While the father walked over to wash his hands, he stopped once again at the end of the stairs to look through the window. He sighed deeply and then whispered a prayer. His faraway look revealed that his heart yearned for something beyond the horizon.

The sun was hiding behind the brown mountains, leaving behind reddish stripes that gave way to purple and dark blue.

It was then that his look focused on a silhouette moving against the grayish background of the road. Though stodgy and slow, it was the same walk of the one who had left. His eyes grew big, and his heart leaped within him. He flung the front door wide open, ran through the garden, swung open the screeching, old gate, and ran down the dusty road as fast as he could.

"My son!" was all he was able to say before hugging him and sealing the encounter with a kiss on his neck as he started to cry like a child.

Looking to the ground, the son, visibly shaking and crying, said, "Father, I have sinned against heaven and against you, and I don't deserve..."

"Shhhh," said the father, placing his fingers upon his son's lips. "Welcome home. I have missed you."

Mercy runs toward you when you want to come back to God, and it runs faster than judgment.

Several years ago I heard Benny Hinn say, "When you take one step toward God, He takes three steps toward you."

When we return, heaven comes down to us with an

embrace, and when we sheepishly look at our home from afar, the Father's embrace leads us back into His love.

THE EMBRACE THAT MAKES YOU FORGET

I went for the first time to Spain in 1993, with my brother-in-law Rodrigo, my sister Guiselle, and two Puerto Rican musicians. After almost three weeks, the tour was about to end with an event near Puente Genil, which is close to Seville.

One morning we received a telephone call from a man by the name of Marcos Zapata, a pastor from the city of Lugo in Galicia, Spain. He was begging us to go visit him. Regretfully, I told him we couldn't accept the invitation because we were booked for another concert and didn't have much free time to rest.

When I talked to my brother-in-law about the call, he told me that he felt we had to go. But there was nothing I could do now; I had hung up the phone, and I didn't know the phone number to call the pastor back. Interestingly, the concert event we had was canceled, which freed us to have a concert at Pastor Zapata's church and still have time to rest.

When we came back late that night, the phone rang. It was Marcos Zapata again. He apologized and said that he was calling in the hopes that something may have happened to allow us to go. (What an incredible guy! Don't you think?)

The next day we drove for nine hours to the city of Lugo. We went on a bus with seventy other passengers, the windows were shut airtight, the air conditioning wasn't working, and the majority of the passengers smoked. Without exaggerating, there was so much smoke that we couldn't even see the driver. We were exhausted, uncomfortable, and irritated.

God's grace is an embrace.

I must confess that I wanted to go back home! I regretted several times having said yes to the pastor.

However, when the bus doors opened up at our destination, we were welcomed with the warmest hug I have ever received despite the rain and the cold. This hug sealed a friendship that I treasure to this day, and everything else was forgotten.

A hug can make a prodigal son forget the shame of eating garbage and walking around like a beggar. It makes the guilt go away and the tiredness to be forgotten. That is the grace of God. It makes us feel loved and welcomed. It opens the heart and says to us, "I have been waiting for you."

God's grace is an embrace.

82

THE RING OF RESTORATION

After the welcome comes the confirmation of his love. The father overflowed with joy upon seeing his son return home. He placed a ring on his son's finger. A ring is a symbol of belonging. It is the Holy Spirit who comes to us in a manifestation of restoration when we dare to cross that bridge of confrontation, confession, and transparency.

That is the process through which the Lord took me when I was in my twenties in order to teach me who I was, to tell me that I belonged to His house, and that I belonged to my Father and my Father belonged to me. My destiny is to worship eternally before His throne.

We have not received the spirit of fear to be slaves, as we were for many years. We have received the spirit of adoption through which we cry out, "Abba Father."

Scripture says, "And [God] put his Spirit in our hearts as a deposit" (2 Cor. 1:22, NIV).

This deposit was given as a pledge or sign of a contract, or the first payment given as guarantee of the full payment of the debt. The Holy Spirit is the seal that assures us that we belong to God. The Holy Spirit is an advance, a deposit, the valid signature on a contract. His presence in our lives ratifies that we have a genuine faith and that we are sons of God. And His power works in us transforming our lives. It is an advance from the total change that we will experience in eternity.

83

That ring symbolizes who we are and to whom we belong. We have a new earth and a new home; we're not strangers, as the Book of the Ephesians says, "Consequently, you are no longer foreigners and aliens, but fellow citizens with God's people and members of God's household" (Eph. 2:19, NIV).

This is the experience of the prodigal son, and it is the discovery that all of us who have a true relationship with God need. This bond is not based on what we have done; rather, it is based upon what He did. The Father has rebuilt the bridge from heaven to earth. He took away sin, rent the veil, and opened the doors of His heart.

This helps us to discover that God's heart is open and that we need only to come in and take all that it is in Him. We allow Him to throw a party for us as we sing and worship Him again. We allow Him to give us new shoes that will help us learn to walk in a new dimension, standing upright once again.

This is what happened to us when we converted, and it happens every time God takes us through a process where we must be more honest and confront the darkness in our hearts in order to be delivered and to walk in more intimate fellowship with God. He gives us new shoes and teaches us to walk.

As this chapter comes to a close, nothing would be more appropriate than to unveil our hearts and confess our lack of passion for God. Why don't you do it with the words of this song, an old one written by Keith Green, which helped to expose the coldness of my soul during my teenage years.

> Lord, the feelings are not the same,
> I guess I'm older, I guess I've changed.
> And how I wish it had been explained,
> That as you're growing you must remember,
> That nothing lasts, except the grace of God,
> By which I stand, in Jesus.
> I know that I would surely fall away,
> Except for grace, by which I'm saved.
>
> Lord, I remember that special way,
> I vowed to serve you, when it was brand new.
> But like Peter, I can't even watch and pray,
> One hour with you, and I bet I could deny you, too.
> But nothing lasts, except the grace of God,
> By which I stand, in Jesus.
> I'm sure that my whole life would waste away,
> Except for grace, by which I'm saved.
> But nothing lasts, except the grace of God,
> By which I stand, in Jesus.
> I know that I would surely fall away,
> Except for grace, by which I'm saved.[1]

Repeat this prayer:

Loving Father, You are the Eternal One who never changes, and You are immutable. I come to You. I have to admit that my soul changes like the leaves with the seasons. My eyes were distracted, my passion grew cold, and my soul has lived in a province distant from You for so long. I am returning to You, where I belong. Let my soul burn with pure fire, let my eyes be cleansed with Your light, let my steps be firm with Your grace, and let my soul rest secure again in You.

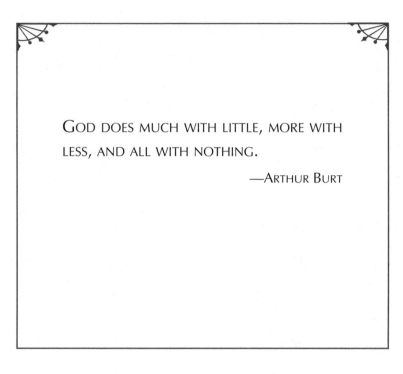

GOD DOES MUCH WITH LITTLE, MORE WITH LESS, AND ALL WITH NOTHING.

—ARTHUR BURT

CHAPTER FIVE

SEEKING THE FATHER'S BLESSING

I N 1992, DURING the Praise and Worship Conference, Chuy Olivares, a pastor and key worship leader in Mexico, ministered in the church I attend. He spoke about God's ways and His divine dealing with His children. After his preaching, Chuy made an altar call. As the conference director, I felt so blessed by the word that I went forward. There I had a short vision in which I saw a fountain of crystal-clear water reflecting the afternoon sun. I presumptuously thought, *That must be my heart.* Then the Holy Spirit added, "You haven't seen the whole picture." I saw the Lord's hand going into the bottom of that fountain and begin searching for something. As He did, the crystal-clear water was stirred and mixed with the stagnant water and leaves that were rising from the bottom. Finally, the fountain of crystal-clear water became muddy. When I saw that image, I cried and said to the Lord, "It can't be that this is my life."

He said to me, "Yes, that's you. I have shown you this because next year I will take you through a process of confrontation, transparency, and repentance."

"But what should I repent from?" I asked in amazement.

"That's what I need for you to discover," He answered.

From that moment on, I entered a new phase of confrontation, but this time it wasn't at the same level as when I was nineteen years old. I discovered that the process that began in my adolescence had not ended; it was incomplete. A crucial time in my life was approaching, and the rest of my Christian walk depended on my response to God's dealing with me.

During 1993, God allowed me to acknowledge my need to stop being a self-sufficient person, as I had been all my Christian life. My formula was, "God and me; I don't need anybody else." I used to tell the Lord that if He needed to deal with me about something to do it directly. "You deal with me, You speak to me, You heal me; I don't need mediators or help," were my words. That is a maxim many people in the church live by, but it is deceiving. None of us were created to change without help. None of us have the absolute truth of

God; therefore, we need that "spark" of God in our brothers and sisters. We were created as people who need to belong to a family, to a house, to a church. In the body of Christ, each one of us has a reflection of Jesus, and we need to share it with one another.

My spiritual independence and my hidden pride would have led me to spiritual failure in the ministry if it weren't because of God's particular dealing with my life during that year. But God forced me to be transparent, and happily, He used some people that became very dear friends during that hard process. I will speak about this more in-depth in chapter seven.

> *None of us have the absolute truth of God; therefore, we need that "spark" of God in our brothers and sisters. We were created as people who need to belong to a family, to a house, to a church.*

Transparency has to do with daring to be ourselves, coming with confidence before a Father who loves us and accepts us for who we are so that He can change us. But it is also necessary to learn to be transparent with those who are God's instruments to bring healing and restoration to our lives.

Discovering the essence of sin in us, be it religiosity, pride, independence, or carnality, is the initial step in accepting God's love and His open arms. Freedom comes when we understand that we can't do it ourselves and that the answer is not in our hands. When we grasp this truth, the gospel, which is the good news of restoration, forgiveness, renewal, and holiness, sets us free. This is the beginning of the path to God's presence.

Spiritual brokenness is necessary for all this to take place, and that was Jacob's experience. In his story are certain life principles for those who are seeking that spiritual transformation.

JACOB'S EXPERIENCE

> When the time came for her to give birth, there were twin boys in her womb. The first to come out was red, and his whole body was like a hairy garment; so they named him Esau.
>
> —GENESIS 25:24–25, NIV

The Bible tells the wonderful story that begins with Isaac, Abraham's son, and Issac's wife, Rebekah, who was barren. After the Lord's intervention, Rebekah became pregnant. But this mother went through a terrible experience during her pregnancy. Her sons were fighting within her womb before they were born. Given the circumstance, she consulted with God about what was happening to her, and He revealed to her that inside of her were two strong personalities, two nations, two peoples who were divided even from the womb. He also told her that one would be stronger than the other and that the older of her sons would serve the younger.

When the time came to give birth, Rebekah had her twins, Esau and Jacob. The first one to be born was red, and they called him Esau, which means "hairy" because his body was covered with hair. Next, the second of the two, Jacob, which means "supplanter" or "one who grabs the heal," was born holding on to his brother's heel.

Jacob was marked from birth by a name that was contemptuous and degrading: "supplanter." This name outlined the intentions of his heart. Jacob always fought for his place and a blessing that did not belong to him. Even before birth, he fought with his twin to be first. However, when Esau emerged first from his mother's womb, Jacob grabbed him by the heel.

Esau soon became his father's favorite because he was an outdoorsman and a skillful hunter. He was his father's pride and joy. Issac loved Esau because he was his firstborn, and Esau became his eyes.

Jacob, on the other hand, was his mother's favorite. The Bible describes him as a quiet man, a tent dweller. He was the "stay-at-home" type; you wouldn't find him out hunting for birds or bothering the neighbors. If he had lived today, he would have lived buried in his books and "surfing the Internet." That's why he was his mother's love.

Two strong and very different personalities. Jacob experienced at an early age the absence of his father's blessing, who preferred his older brother. Jacob, however, was raised not to think as being the last but the first.

As Jacob grew up, he tried to take the blessing from the family's firstborn, and he accomplished that by taking advantage of his older brother in a moment of weakness. He obtained the birthright in exchange for a bowl of lentil stew.

> Once when Jacob was cooking some stew, Esau came in from the open country, famished. He said to Jacob, "Quick, let me have some of that red stew! I'm famished!" ... Jacob replied, "First sell me your birthright." ... So he swore an oath to him, selling his birthright to Jacob. ... So Esau despised his birthright.
>
> —GENESIS 25:29–34

Esau was a person who lacked spiritual discernment. He lived by his instincts and desires. Jacob, on the other hand, accomplished his goal by buying with lentil stew the spiritual blessing that he so desired.

Jacob didn't get to be the firstborn, but he obtained the birthright and the blessing. The firstborn son in a Jewish family enjoys benefits that the other sons do not. According to the Law, the firstborn son in a family was to be offered to the Lord. He was the firstfruits of a married couple, so he had to be given to God and redeemed. That's why for the parents to be able to retain their son instead of offering him to God in service, they had to redeem him. They raised their son, but they dedicated him to the Lord as an offering of service. The firstborn also had the possibility of receiving the patriarch's blessing when he grew up. Once his father died, the firstborn was the successor. Esau would inherit 60 percent of his father's possessions, and he would be the leader or the chief.

Because of all this, it was so important for Jacob to obtain the blessing his father would give to Esau, his twin older brother.

THE DECEPTION

When these two brothers grew up and Isaac, their father, was about to die, something very important happened. Esau was about to receive the patriarchal blessing from his father, but before that took place, Isaac asked Esau to go hunting and prepare him a special dish.

Rebekah was listening behind the door. Immediately she called her favorite son, Jacob, and told him that Isaac was about to bless Esau. She knew that somehow Jacob desired that blessing. Jacob accepted the deceitful strategy that his mother proposed to him to obtain his father's blessing. Then, he quickly prepared a soup and disguised himself as his brother:

Then Rebekah took the best clothes of Esau her older son, which she had in the house, and put them on her younger son Jacob. She also covered his hands and the smooth part of his neck with the goatskins. Then she handed to her son Jacob the tasty food and the bread she had made. He went to his father and said, "My father." "Yes, my son," he answered. "Who is it?" Jacob said to his father, "I am Esau your firstborn. I have done as you told me. Please sit up and eat some of my game so that you may give me your blessing." Isaac asked his son, "How did you find it so quickly, my son?" "The LORD your God gave me success," he replied. Then Isaac said to Jacob, "Come near so I can touch you, my son, to know whether you really are my son Esau or not." Jacob went close to his father Isaac, who touched him and said, "The voice is the voice of Jacob, but the hands are the hands of Esau." He did not recognize him, for his hands were hairy like those of his brother Esau; so he blessed him. "Are you really my son Esau?" he asked. "I am," he replied. Then he said, "My son, bring me some of your game to eat, so that I may give you my blessing." Jacob brought it to him and he ate; and he brought some wine and he drank. Then his father Isaac said to him, "Come here, my son, and kiss me." So he went to him and kissed him. When

Isaac caught the smell of his clothes, he blessed him and said, "Ah, the smell of my son is like the smell of a field that the LORD has blessed. May God give you of heaven's dew and of earth's richness—an abundance of grain and new wine. May nations serve you and peoples bow down to you. Be lord over your brothers, and may the sons of your mother bow down to you. May those who curse you be cursed and those who bless you be blessed."

—GENESIS 27:15–29, NIV

Jacob achieved his dream through deception, supplanting, usurping, and lying. Jacob reflects a generation that is willing to do anything necessary to obtain the blessing of a father who was never there.

THE JACOB GENERATION

Jacob was a child who sought his father's blessing. This generation, like the Latin American generation, is the fruit of unknown fathers, a generation that doesn't know their father or his heart.

We are the result of a generation that attempts to buy their children's happiness with material things—cars, good colleges, and fun weekends—but trying to buy them these things does not let them know their father's heart. It is a generation of men who do not know how to love or how to communicate. Latin America is the fruit of a generation of men who hide behind alcohol. Men who shaped a generation of rejected children, who do not have an identity, who do not know their value, and who are seeking a blessing. That is the Jacob generation.

The fruit of this generation desperately seeks to hear a blessing but never does hear it. This is the reason why they substitute with religious, perfectionist tendencies. They confuse success with materialism, whereas others who don't overcome this frustration drown themselves in sin, drugs, and alcohol, repeating the generational curse.

THE FAMILY SPLITS

As Jacob came out, he rejoiced with his mother. A few minutes later, Esau came in the house, and when he realized that he had been deceived, he felt so mocked that he sought to kill Jacob, but Jacob had already escaped. Thus begins a new phase in Jacob's life: he had already accomplished his goal and now began a process of confrontation.

> Isaac trembled violently and said, "Who was it, then, that hunted game and brought it to me? I ate it just before you came and I blessed him—and indeed he will be blessed!"
>
> —GENESIS 27:33, NIV

Isaac understood the power of his words upon the lives of his sons. It is the blessing of a change.

Esau said, "Isn't he rightly named Jacob? He has deceived me these two times: He took my birthright, and now he's taken my blessing!" Then he asked, "Haven't you reserved any blessing for me?"

—GENESIS 27:36, NIV

Esau went out to seek revenge, and from that moment on, the brothers were separated. Finally, Isaac understood God's design, so he blessed Jacob and sent him off, saying:

So Isaac called for Jacob and blessed him and commanded him: "Do not marry a Canaanite woman. Go at once to Paddan Aram, to the house of your mother's father Bethuel. Take a wife for yourself there, from among the daughters of Laban, your mother's brother. May God Almighty bless you and make you fruitful and increase your numbers until you become a community of peoples. May he give you and your descendants the blessing given to Abraham, so that you may take possession of the land where you now live as an alien, the land God gave to Abraham."

—GENESIS 28:1–4, NIV

Jacob obtained his father's blessing through deceit, and because of that, Jacob served Laban. When his father-in-law deceived him, after he had served him seven years to marry Rachel (who was supplanted by Leah), Jacob was forced to work another seven years to be able to enjoy his beloved.

Jacob's problems began there. He had to deal with his own father-in-law's envy, and, in that moment, began God's special dealing with Jacob. God's dealings took Jacob to a point that today shows us the way to follow Him and be transformed.

[MY] RESPONSIBILITY . . . IS TO "LET GO AND LET GOD"—TO GET OUT OF THE WAY—MY ONLY STRUGGLE, A STRUGGLE NOT TO STRUGGLE.[1]

—ARTHUR BURT

CHAPTER SIX

THE MARK OF GOD

THE SPIRITUAL PROCESS that leads us to experience holiness is one in which two essential elements converge. The first one is the grace of God that touches us and imparts to us a Christlikeness. The second is our will that yields to the Lord and moves us to make the necessary decisions to accomplish the changes we desire.

We will never reach the heights of that level of holiness without Him being the one to impart it. The perfect work of Christ on the cross is the source from which such blessing flows. His sacrifice for our sins and His victorious resurrection assure believers the joy of tasting mercy (an expression of divine character) during our present life.

This, however, does not eliminate our responsibility to seek holiness and spiritual transformation. We are collaborators with God in this process. By the same grace we receive from God, we respond to His call to walk in holiness and restoration.

Young Jacob sought his father's blessing and finally found it. To get it, he deceived his family. His search was sincere; he wanted to break from the stigma that his name implied, which was an expression of his spiritual misery and corrupt character.

Once he heard Isaac's blessing, Jacob was sent to look for a wife. God's favor was on him, blessing him in all areas, but the moment came when the Lord called him to come back to his parents' house. The "supplanter" comes to a crossroads to obtain the change.

I want to invite you to observe the six steps that you can take to discover an intimate relationship with God and a place of healing for your soul. The following principles revolutionized my life and were an important part of the divine strategy to bring me to a place of maturity and peace.

1. Close the unfinished chapters.

> Then the LORD said to Jacob, "Go back to the land of your fathers and to your relatives, and I will be with you."
> —GENESIS 31:3, NIV

In order to heal the emotional breaches and discover true freedom, we will have to understand the "place" in our lives where we were marked. It is possible that this "mark" was caused in our own home. Life works in such a way that you cannot reach maturity unless you resolve the place of your beginning.

In order to reach God's potential for you, you have to identify the unfinished chapters of your childhood and adolescence with the purpose of mending the mistakes and healing the wounds.

The story of our race was decided tragically in the Garden of Eden, because in that place man decided to do his own will and to break his relationship with the Creator. In order to change the course of our history, God had to go back to a garden (Gethsemane) in which Jesus (the God-man) took our place to submit us once again to God's will.

During the Christmas of 1995, we had a family reunion around dinner. Oscar, my older brother, and his wife, as well as my sister, Guiselle, and Rodrigo, my brother-in-law, and I spent a very special time.

The phone rang, and Oscar took the call. I soon realized it was Dad who wanted to greet us. I signaled to my brother to allow me to talk to him. After greeting him, I invited him to come, to which he replied negatively. I had to insist that he would have no problems with Mom and that it was me who wanted to see him at home. Even though we hadn't lived with him for over ten years, Dad used to visit us occasionally.

Finally, he came and ate with us. While we ate, I recognize the Lord's voice asking me to obey Him. Many months before I began to feel the need to talk to my dad to take care of some unresolved issues in our lives, and the Lord had indicated that He would give me the moment. A few minutes after we finished eating, Dad told us that he was leaving right away. I offered to take him home.

Although at the beginning it was a bit difficult, as we got closer to his house we were able to have a sincere and deep conversation. Dad thanked me for being in charge of the family and apologized for not helping me as he should have. To my amazement, he opened his heart, telling me the details of the crisis that ended his marriage.

> *The process of giving and receiving forgiveness seals what God desires to do so that we grow and start a new phase in our lives as princes with God, as people who rule and reach maturity in the Lord.*

I had before me a repentant man, and before him was one who felt compassion. It was our first man-to-man conversation.

106

"Son, I am indebted to you and your brothers and sister," he said at the end.

"Dad," I said to him, "you don't owe us anything. There is One who already paid that debt for you. All of us at home love you and have forgiven you. Everything is forgotten."

I hugged him, and we said good-bye. An important chapter in my life was closed that Christmas Eve.

The process of giving and receiving forgiveness seals what God desires to do so that we grow and start a new phase in our lives as princes with God, as people who rule and reach maturity in the Lord.

2. Accept other people's confrontations.

Jacob knew that going back home to his family meant facing Esau. His brother was the sum of his mistakes and the personification of the weaknesses of character with which he struggled. God brought Esau as a messenger of confrontation.

> When the messengers returned to Jacob, they said, "We went to your brother Esau, and now he is coming to meet you, and four hundred men are with him." In great fear and distress Jacob divided the people.... Then Jacob prayed, "O God of my father Abraham...Save me, I pray, from the hand of my brother Esau, for I am afraid he will come and attack me."
> —Genesis 32:6–11, NIV

God allowed Jacob to be confronted by his past mistakes. God used two people to accomplish that purpose: Esau and Laban.

People and circumstances alone don't change what is in our hearts. The change is produced by our attitude when facing that confrontation.

Often the people closest to us are the tools that the enemy uses to hurt us. But those with whom we deal on a daily basis are also the divine messengers of confrontation. We don't ask for them; in fact, if we could, we would get rid of them.

A poor woman desperate by the agony of a miserable life beside her husband prayed, "Lord, either You take him, or I'll send him to You." Many times when we pray for God to change the person who irritates us, we receive the answer from the divine finger pointing at us and saying, "It is you who needs to change the most."

There's another way in which we can benefit from confrontation. The Bible teaches us in Proverbs 27:17 that friends are God's instruments to polish our character. "As iron sharpens iron, so one man sharpens another" (NIV).

We all need friends and ministers on whom we can count to hold us accountable. One of the greatest needs that we as God's servants have is to establish bonds with godly men and women who share our struggles and from whom we receive

108

counsel and exhortation. If we want change, we need to put aside isolating ourselves spiritually and learn to trust others. We will discuss this more in the following chapter.

3. Discover God in your solitude.

Jacob decided to divide his people. He sent them as caravans before him with gifts for Esau, trying to find grace before his brother. Then he found himself alone:

> So Jacob was left alone...
> —GENESIS 32:24, NIV

The most transcendent things in the life of a man take place when he is alone in God's presence. The best school of change is not found in the multitude of a conference or in the social life of the church.

Moses spent years "alone" in the desert, and there he had an encounter with God. Similarly, David learned to be a worshiper through his long vigils in solitude. Hannah was barren until she decided to go alone to the temple and bare her soul in God's presence, and there, in "solitude," she found peace and change. Likewise, Jesus was tempted in His "solitude," but there He also obtained victory for us.

We need to find our Lord who is in solitude.

> But when you pray, go into your room, close the door and *pray to your Father, who is unseen.* Then your

> Father, who sees what is done in secret, will reward
> you.
> —MATTHEW 6:6, NIV, EMPHASIS ADDED

Christianity promises to place us where our father Adam lost the battle so that we recover what was lost. There we will open our eyes, and before us we will find the Father's great big eyes looking at us in amazement, like the first time Adam saw Him. Alone, face-to-face, we will see our image reflected in His eyes, and He, smiling, will seek His image in our look, just like a father who, looking at his newborn son for the first time, cries when he discovers his resemblance in the baby's face.

Praying alone is the place where we come to know the Father who is in secret, and at the same time we discover that we are His beloved children.

> After six days Jesus took Peter, James and John with
> him and led them up a high mountain, where they were
> all alone. There he was transfigured before them. His
> clothes became dazzling white, whiter than anyone in
> the world could bleach them.... Then a cloud appeared
> and enveloped them, and a voice came from the cloud:
> "This is my Son, whom I love."
> —MARK 9:2–3, 7, NIV

Luke adds:

As he was praying, the appearance of his face changed.
—LUKE 9:29, NIV

Jesus went to the mountain to pray, and three of the disciples went with Him. As Jesus prayed, His facial appearance began to change, and He began reflecting who He really was, leaving His earthly appearance behind.

> *Praying alone is the place where we come to know the Father who is in secret, and at the same time we discover that we are His beloved children.*

When we enter into fellowship with God, we begin to reflect who we really are and what is on the inside of us: God's presence. Consequently, we discover our true worth.

We all have difficulty feeling at ease when we're alone. Maybe we hate loneliness because we fear being with the person we hate the most in this world: ourselves. This happens because we have not mended things with the person we see in the mirror every morning. That's why it is necessary to come to God, who helps us to accept ourselves just as we are and to value ourselves as He values us.

4. Yield completely to God.

The last and primary struggle Jacob had was at Peniel.

...and a man wrestled with him till daybreak. When the man saw that he could not overpower him, he touched the socket of Jacob's hip so that his hip was wrenched as he wrestled with the man. Then the man said, "Let me go, for it is daybreak." But Jacob replied, "I will not let you go unless you bless me."

—Genesis 32:24–26, NIV

Jacob prepared to fight with all his strength. What else could he do? Fighting was all he knew. Perhaps the "supplanter" said, "Good or bad, I have gotten to this point fighting, and if I am going to advance to the next chapter, I'll do it in the same way, even if I have to fight with God Himself." And that's exactly what he was doing.

When we admit our weakness and human limitation, we open the door to God's power. Only there the natural man is broken and gives way to God.

Before him was the last resource, his only hope. Somehow, Jacob understood that the blessing couldn't come from his brother's or his father's hand, but that it had to come from God Himself. But the fight itself was not the way to bring about change.

When the man saw that he could not overpower him,

he touched the socket of Jacob's hip so that his hip was
wrenched as he wrestled with the man.
—GENESIS 32:25, NIV

God had to hurt the fighter in order to humble him.

Brokenness is the only thing that heals us from religion
and throws us to the ground, humbled, saying, "I can't
do anything in my own strength." The person who fights
thinks he can obtain it, and that's why he fights. The Pharisee fought with everybody, with himself, and even with his
God to show that he could reach holiness by himself. But
his pride left him in spiritual misery.

Peniel, however, is the place where the person recognizes
that he is not able and is prostrated, waiting on God. When
we admit our weakness and human limitation, we open the
door to God's power. Only there the natural man is broken
and gives way to God. That is called total surrender and
consecration: when we abandon ourselves totally in God's
hands.

It is imperative that we accept the fact of being annulled,
reduced to nothing, so that God may be all in us.

Again I quote Arthur Burt, who says, "God does much
with little, more with less, and all with nothing."

Singer and songwriter Wes King describes this moment
with a wonderful skill in his song "Magnificent Defeat":[2]

What is my purpose
For being here
I've had no burning bush or voices in my ear
I have been wandering
All these years
But I've seen no manna
Or angels appear.

Now I long for the solace of my soul.
I have wandered from pole to pole
Here I lie
Broken at your feet
Rejoicing at
This magnificent defeat.

I have been wrestling
All through the night
The darkness hides the face
Of the one I fight.
Beloved enemy
Demands my life and all I am
But then he blesses me
And gives it back again.

5. Dare to confess.

The man asked him, "What is your name?" "Jacob," he
answered.

—GENESIS 32:27, NIV

Where are you? What have you done? Who are you? What is your name? These are the divine questions to a race that hides behind a bush just as Adam did.

Nonetheless, God invites us to come out of hiding and be transparent. He seeks to confront us so that we confess. He asks us if we have the guts to admit who we are and what is happening to us, if we have the courage to speak our name.

Brennan Manning, author of the outstanding book *Abba's Child: The Cry of the Heart for Intimate Belonging*, tells us how crucial is our decision at this crossroads:

> *What is your struggle? Are you able to admit your problem? If you can confess who you are, what is happening to you, and what makes you suffer, then God can deliver you.*

> When I fell I had two options: To go back to the guilt, the fear, and depression; or to run to my Heavenly Father's arms. To choose to live as a victim of my sickness, or to decide to trust in Abba's unchanging love.[3]

What is your struggle? Are you able to admit your problem? Can you take responsibility for the evil with which you are struggling? If you can confess who you are, what is happening to you, and what makes you suffer, then God can deliver you. The need for transparency and for admitting our vulnerability is a principle of life. We must recognize our imperfection.

Jacob could have said, "My father never loved me," or "Esau is a fool." You can continue blaming your parents, your country, or your bad luck, but as long as you repeat Adam and Eve's words, "It was the serpent," you won't be transformed.

The honest confession before God is the starting point for His powerful intervention to take place in us. On the other hand, confession before our brothers and sisters is the channel through which we come out of the darkness that is in our hearts and receive the healing light of God.

Confession has been a key point in my life. I was literally forced to define who, in essence, I am and confess it before God, before a friend, and before a brother.

Confession was also important in Jonah's life. While he was trapped in the belly of a fish for three days, isolated in his self-sufficiency, he recognized that sin was trapping him. Then he recognized and said, "I will fulfill my vows to the Lord. I give up; I will do what You say." And at that moment the fish spat him up on a beach.

You need to accept and confess. Identify yourself with

Jesus in order to be free. In Isaiah 53, Isaiah calls Him the "Suffering Servant," a "man of sorrows, and familiar with suffering," not hiding His wounds but showing them, because when He shows them He brings freedom to other people.

Admit, confess, speak, and seek help. "But everything exposed by the light becomes visible, for it is light that makes everything visible" (Eph. 5:13–14, NIV).

Confession is the only thing that allows the darkness to be exposed to the light and turns into liberty and healing. That was how Jacob admitted his identity, his sin, and began his change.

But he said to the Lord, "My name is the supplanter."

After we confess, we enter a totally different spiritual dimension.

6. Let God mark you.

> Then the man said, "Your name will no longer be Jacob, but Israel, because you have struggled with God and with men and have overcome."...So Jacob called the place Peniel, saying, "It is because I saw God face to face, and *yet my life was spared.*"
> —GENESIS 32:28, 30, EMPHASIS ADDED

After seeing God face-to-face, your soul will be free. God has a new name for those who walk through the bridge of confrontation, who travel through the narrow road of confession, and who come to the altar of total surrender.

To the extent that we come to God daily and identify ourselves with Jesus and His work, our internal appearance will begin to reveal the glory of His presence. Our soul will find rest in the new identity brought to us by the new name given to us. The supplanter left behind his shame, and now he was called "Israel."

God says to you that your name will no longer be unworthy, impure, or perverse. He has in His presence a new name for you, a new nature for your life. He says to you: "You are My beloved child; you are the apple of My eyes. You are My special treasure, a diadem on My forehead. You are My palace; you are the temple of My spirit. You are My Zion; you are the land I desired, the New Jerusalem, the city where I will live forever. That is your new name. Discover it. You are no longer anonymous; you are My child, My family. Before you were a coward; now you are a warrior."

> Jacob said, "Please tell me your name." But he replied, "Why do you ask my name?" Then *he blessed him there.*
> —GENESIS 32:29, NIV, EMPHASIS ADDED

This is the good news, the words that the generation of silence of our parents could not communicate, but that now God announces to us. It is our new identity in God, which

118

is expressed in each word coming out of His mouth and written in the Bible.

> But now, this is what the LORD says—he who created you, O Jacob, he who formed you, O Israel: "Fear not, for I have redeemed you; I have summoned you by name; you are mine.... Since you are precious and honored in my sight, and because I love you, I will give men in exchange for you, and people in exchange for your life."
>
> —ISAIAH 43:1, 4, NIV

Let these words come alive in you when you come to Peniel. While you wait there, allow God to remove the names that the enemy has given you, and instead, allow Him to seal you with His mark of love.

> The sun rose above him as he passed Peniel, and *he was limping because of his hip.*
>
> —GENESIS 32:31, NIV, EMPHASIS ADDED

> But Esau ran to meet Jacob and embraced him; he threw his arms around his neck and kissed him. And they wept.
>
> —GENESIS 33:4, NIV

Two are better than one, because they have a good return for their work: If one falls down, his friend can help him up. But pity the man who falls and has no one to help him up!...Though one may be overpowered, two can defend themselves. A cord of three strands is not quickly broken.

—Ecclesiastes 4:9–10, 12, NIV

CHAPTER SEVEN

TWO ARE BETTER...

N NOVEMBER OF 1992 I attended a worship conference in Guatemala City, Guatemala. Daniel Argüijo, the guitarist who accompanied me, talked to me a lot about a couple he had met during those days who had impacted him.

We had so much to do that I couldn't meet them until after the conference. That night while we waited for the meeting to get started, Juan Carlos Alvarado, the event leader, asked us to greet some of the people who were around us. When I turned around, there was a couple next to me, and I greeted them. When I hugged them I felt a great peace and love.

"You have to be a pastor," I told him.

"How do you know?" he responded, surprised.

"Only a person with the heart of a pastor can hug like that," I replied confidently.

After we laughed for a while, he introduced himself, "I am Rey Matos, and this is Mildred, my wife."

Immediately, I realized that this was the couple that Daniel had talked so much about to me. I felt as if we had known each other all our lives.

The next day we went for a stroll around Lake Atitlán; later we went sailing for a few hours, and we had a wonderful time together. That afternoon a wonderful friendship was born. Eight months later, in July of 1993, I visited Puerto Rico for the first time in response to an invitation to the first worship conference that the Matoses had organized.

One of my prayers at that time in my life was that I would be able to establish friendships with people to whom I could become accountable.

In September of 1993 during my second visit to the Matos' home, the circumstances in my life that year led me to start that kind of accountability with Rey. We sat on the front porch of his house around midnight, and we talked until six in the morning. For the first time in my life, I opened my heart to someone else and allowed that someone to see my struggles, my mistakes, and my fears. While Rey listened to my story, I felt as if a weight had been lifted from me, and my soul began to look out at the light of God.

124

When I was finished talking, I looked at him timidly, not knowing what reaction my words would provoke. However, I found the last thing I was expecting: a look of love, acceptance, and hope. It was the healing look of God the Father. Rey shared my burdens, understood my fears, and offered me a hand, telling me, "You're not alone. We're going to come out ahead of this together."

Rey's friendship enriched my life tremendously with the sincerity and the confrontation of a brother and with the timely wisdom of a father.

As part of the process to which God had introduced me, I sought out to establish this kind of relationship with my pastors in Costa Rica. In look-

> *It is necessary to open our hearts and trust other people in order to receive from them what God wants to do in our lives.*

ing for their support, I found the same, loving response. Today, both Raúl Vargas and Eric Linox know about my struggles, my difficulties, and everything about my life. They are my support in prayer, wisdom, and counsel on a personal level as well as on a ministry level. All of this happened after that long conversation with Rey Matos.

It is necessary to open our hearts and trust other people

in order to receive from them what God wants to do in our lives. If a great deal of the pain we carry is caused by others, then God will use other human beings to heal those hurts.

In the biblical narrative of 1 Samuel we read that Eli was beside Hannah in her moment of crisis, and he was the instrument to give her a word of blessing: "May God bless you and give you the desire of your heart." Hannah heard God's voice on the lips of the priest and returned home changed.

God uses friendship and the presence of His children around us to accomplish various purposes in us:

1. To make His voice and His blessings tangible and evident to us

2. To help us carry the emotional and spiritual load with which we are dealing

3. To supply our lack of paternal and brotherly love (The church is an instrument of redemption and restoration through its members. For example, we men are called to provide the paternal figure that orphans need, the children of the widow, the street kids, and the homeless young people.)

4. To confront sin in us and to prevent us from falling in it: Samuel confronted Saul's error (1 Sam. 15:10–24); Paul rebukes the inconsistent conduct of

Peter, his colleague (Gal. 2:11–12); Nathan, one of David's best friends and close companion, confronts the king's sin and, in so doing, delivers him from destruction (2 Sam. 12:1–13).

Faithful are the wounds of a friend.

—Proverbs 27:6

5. To give us direction and wisdom through counsel

Poverty and shame shall be to him that refuseth instruction: but he that regardeth reproof shall be honoured.

—Proverbs 13:18

He who listens to a life-giving rebuke will be at home among the wise.

—Proverbs 15:31, NIV

Perfume and incense bring joy to the heart, and the pleasantness of one's friend springs from his earnest counsel.

—Proverbs 27:9, NIV

OF FOXES AND FRIENDSHIPS

I want to share a story that may illustrate the importance of having friends.

One afternoon while I was working in my home office, I asked Flor, my secretary, to go to the next room and find me a ream of paper.

A few minutes later, I heard a scream. I jumped from my chair to see what was going on and saw her coming toward me, saying, "There's an animal trapped in that room!"

"What animal?" I asked, because we didn't have pets in the house.

"An animal with sharp teeth; you have to get it out of there," she said, surprised.

I hope there isn't any animal there, I thought, *because I don't want to have to get it.*

I grabbed a broom, opened the door to the room, and began to move the reams of paper stored there. What a surprise I got when a big black nose wanted to attack the broom! It was what in Costa Rica we call a "fox," dark gray, with a very long nose and mouselike tail that's about ten inches long. A horrible animal! I stepped back, and when I hit it, it ran away and hid underneath a piece of furniture.

Then Flor went to get a blackboard to block the entrance door and keep the animal from escaping. In that moment a thought crossed my mind: *This animal is trapped in this room, and we are trapped with it.*

I began hitting the furniture without stopping so it would get out, but it jumped on me angrily. I hit it and threw it against the wall. It tried to go out the window but couldn't, so it attacked me again.

I hit it with the broom, but the animal wouldn't budge.

128

Then it ran to the door where Flor was. It was then that I hit it over the head until I finally knocked it down. We put it in a box and closed it. Juan Carlos, my assistant and friend, began (desperately) to seal that box with tape so that the fox wouldn't escape.

When we picked up the box to take it out to the street, the terrible animal escaped through a hole in the corner of the box that was not sealed. That kind of animal is very slippery and fits through spaces we think they can't.

> *Friends are like a rearview mirror of a car because they help protect us from the blind spots as we drive.*

It ran again toward the door where my secretary was standing. I again attacked it with the broom and hit it so hard that it flew through the air and landed right on top of Juan Carlos.

All I can remember is Juan Carlos' face. He turned totally red, his eyes bulging, and he screamed, "O my God!" I will never forget that expression of panic. The funny thing is that my friends later told me my face had that same horrifed expression when the animal attacked me.

Finally, I knocked it down, and we got it in the box again.

After closing the box very well, we got rid of it. (Don't ask me how...)

A few days later the Lord showed us that this whole experience had an important purpose. This precious friendship that I have had with Juan Carlos and his family for more than eighteen years had to go into a deeper phase. The Lord called my friend not only to be a key member of my ministry but also a spiritual support to share my burdens.

Juan Carlos is another one of those people from God to whom I have given permission to speak into my life. He is someone who has placed himself in God's hands to help me "get rid" of anything that may hinder the flow of the divine purpose in my life.

Charles Swindoll says in his book *Dropping Your Guard* that friends are like a rearview mirror of a car because they help protect us from the blind spots as we drive. That means that they help us minimize the risk of tripping and falling.

"Catch for us the foxes, the little foxes that ruin the vineyards" (Song of Solomon 2:15, NIV).

A FATHER TO THE FATHERLESS...IS GOD IN HIS HOLY DWELLING.

—PSALM 68:5, NIV

CHAPTER EIGHT

THE EMBRACE OF THE FATHER

I BEGAN THIS BOOK by sharing the experience I had with God when I was nineteen years old. When I sensed His love searching for me without ceasing, I came back, surrendering at His feet. I had such a thirst for God's presence that I would spend hours in prayer and worship daily. I learned to wait quietly on God.

The Holy Spirit taught me to follow His lead in prayer, and little by little, I immersed myself in the delightful depth of worship. I spent hours prostrated in prayer and singing and dancing before God. Often I searched the Scriptures to hear the Father speak to me, and when I did that, He would show me the meaning of that new name He had given me. It was the image that He had of me and that He had recorded carefully in His Word so that I would learn it. The Book of Isaiah became a powerful source of renewal for my thoughts and a comfort for my soul.

One afternoon while I was worshiping the Lord, I presented to Him a complaint. One of the dynamics of worship that I discovered was that I could sit down and have a conversation with God and sometimes ask Him certain things.

King David said:

> One thing I ask of the LORD, this is what I seek: that I may dwell in the house of the LORD all the days of my life, to gaze upon the beauty of the LORD and to seek him in his temple.
>
> —PSALM 27:4, NIV

The word *seek* means to "ask, investigate, to inquire into something." That is what I was doing that afternoon before the Lord. I was asking the Lord, "Lord, why did You allow certain difficult situations in my family? Where were You when I was going through those moments? Why didn't our family have the father figure we needed?"

While I was praying, I began to relive images of one of the hardest situations I lived in my childhood. I saw myself in my room sleeping, when I heard my mother's fragile voice saying, "Danilo, Danilo, wake up!"

134

I got up from the old blue cot that was in the far right corner of my room. The poundings coming from the kitchen shook the old wooden walls.

I saw a chair flying in front of me. Within a few seconds my child's mind figured out what was going on. Then I saw Dad leaving fast and slamming the door so hard that I thought the house would collapse. I ran to the kitchen, and everything was broken, including the glass in the oven door. Everything was a big mess; something terrible had happened.

When I turned to look for Mom, I saw that she was crying and asking for help while holding my younger brother, who was only two or three years old at the time. I realized that it was just another one of those nightmares you have while daydreaming. It wasn't the first time, nor would it be the last, because every time my father drank, he would lose it and take out his anger on Mom.

My mom's pajamas were stained with blood because of a broken nose.

I sat on the cot wishing I was an adult so I could hit my father. But at the same time a terrible fear and a great sensation of helplessness gripped me, and I started crying desperately.

I remember my mom sitting on my bed telling me what happened. It was six o'clock in the morning, and she was awake—as she usually was—getting my brothers and sister ready for school. While the water percolated in a silver coffeepot, she would wash clothes by hand in the reddish concrete kitchen sink.

She heard the clanging of the keys entering the door lock. She suspected it was my dad, since his job kept him out of the house almost all night, and afterward he would frequently spend hours with his friends playing cards. When he entered the house, Mom knew he was drunk because she could hear him stumble as he walked.

After crossing the hallway, he passed by the bedrooms and came to the kitchen, which was at the end of the house. He touched my mother on the shoulder, and she didn't respond. Things between them were bad, and she had no intention of talking to him. When he insisted on getting her attention, she turned to him to see what he wanted. That's when he punched her in the nose, and she had a large, open wound.

My mom ran out to the small dirt patio that looked toward the street. She turned the door handle and moved the metal gate to go get help. She knew Dad had lost it. However, she stopped when she recognized her attempts were futile. We lived in a neighborhood where gossip spread very fast; you couldn't have a sincere friend. The shame forced her to return to the house. That's when she took my younger brother in her arms and entered the house again. Then Dad pushed her on the bed and decided to leave.

136

As I remembered what had happened that morning, I cried a lot, and I asked the Lord again, "What happened? Where were You? Why did You allow my dad to be an alcoholic, and all of this to happen?"

The Lord answered, "You haven't seen the whole picture. Why don't you keep remembering?"

I continued with my eyes closed and relived the situation all over again. I saw my bedroom from left to right. I saw myself from behind, crying on the bed. I could see the sunlight shining through the small window in front of me. I heard my dad slam the door as he left and my mother's sobbing, which blended with my own.

"Keep looking to your right," said the Lord.

There, beside me, I saw Him extending His arm over me while I cried in silence.

"I was there all along," He said to me tenderly. "You didn't know Me yet. You didn't know about Me, but I was always with you. I am the Father you need. This is the time for you to find in Me what you couldn't find in your family."

> *There is no circumstance that His love doesn't know and that His comfort cannot heal. When you perceive His love, all resentment loses its power, and forgiveness blossoms.*

In the embrace of the Father my pain faded away.

There is no circumstance that His love doesn't know and that His comfort cannot heal. When you perceive His love, all resentment loses its power, and forgiveness blossoms.

That was one of the most powerful experiences that I lived in the presence of God, and it healed the deepest parts of my life.

THINK ABOUT HER STORY AND ABOUT YOUR FUTURE

God's revelation as my Father is renewed and becomes deeper, taking new forms as the years go by. As this happens, I enjoy the stability and spiritual rest that faith in Him alone can bring. In fact, God's hand becomes more real and tangible as I go on in life, only now the experience is not so much emotional but goes beyond; it even goes to my spirit.

One of the most difficult times for our family was my mother's death. She had been hospitalized unexpectedly, and after having gone through a very delicate surgical procedure, she survived ten days until she passed away on September 13, 1996. There are no words to describe how painful this situation was for us.

When I remember that process, I realize just how real the heavenly Father's presence was in the midst of it all. While I was writing this chapter, I opened the pages of a small journal I used to keep many years ago. In it I wrote the words that the Lord would give me in some crucial moments. Even though I have never been very good with keeping a journal, I have to admit that I benefited from remembering God's promises.

What you are about to read is what I wrote six months after my mother went to be with the Lord. This records what happened the night before her death. While I walked down the hospital's cold halls, I stopped to look through the windows that faced toward the mountains of the capital, and suddenly I could feel the Lord's presence beside me.

> *I could hear the beeping of the machines down the hall. It was midnight, and while everything is dark, the nurses come and go.*
>
> *Motherhood is dying. You want to do it all and you can't do a thing.*
>
> *You think…images of a distant childhood. You go over life but through the eyes of a mother. You ask yourself how was it all for her. The scarcity and the loneliness. The dreams of being a mother and the disillusion of being alone…the first boy, the first steps, the first Christmas, the first school day.*
>
> *The first graduation…the first salary…the first girl… the first wedding and the first grandchild.*
>
> *You think, you think while the night becomes day…*
>
> *And, again, the smell of chlorine of the hospital, the machines beeping, a respirator, and the struggle of a life slipping away…*

I felt the touch of a warm hand on my shoulder, and I heard His voice. "I think about you and about her; tonight I have you on My thoughts...everything is going to be all right."

In the embrace of the Father we find the strength to walk through the valley of the shadow of death, without fear.

> Is Ephraim my dear son? is he a pleasant child? for since I spake against him, *I do earnestly remember him still*: therefore my bowels are troubled for him; I will surely have mercy upon him, saith the LORD.
> —JEREMIAH 31:20, EMPHASIS ADDED

THE FATHER'S CELEBRATION

As part of the many adjustments that came with Mom's departure, I moved from the house in which we had lived for ten years to another one where I would live by myself. It would be a temporary stay because I never finished settling there. I think that my house/office was a good illustration of the transition process I experienced.

One rainy afternoon in June, I received an unexpected visit from a pastor and very dear friend: Hanz Morúa. Chance meetings are part of this brother's lifestyle, because we have never planned these times of fellowship, but the good thing is that Hanz always appears at the right time. My friend brings with him the freshness of the Holy Spirit expressed in his prayer and in the constant joy that he radiates.

Hanz went to the living room and told me that he wanted to pray for me, but instead of praying, he started crying, and he hugged me. Immediately I could sense God's presence filling that living room, and while I too started crying, the voice of the Lord through him said, "I cover you; I am lifting up your countenance...you have said that I would leave you." My friend smiled and continued, "No, I am here, and, in fact, I am anointing you with an anointing of fire, which is a circle around your life to protect you. You have desired to be in a family, and that is exactly what I desire for you; you will always be in a family. I'm a Father to you, and as such I will do it. I am here to see you reach success and to celebrate with you."

In the embrace of the Father we find the strength to walk through the valley of the shadow of death, without fear.

God visited me in June and allowed me to cry on His shoulder.

> So do not fear, for I am with you; do not be dismayed, for I am your God. I will strengthen you and help you; I will uphold you with my righteous right hand.
> —ISAIAH 41:10, NIV

141

The eternal God is thy refuge, and underneath are the everlasting arms.

—DEUTERONOMY 33:27

Above is the everlasting God, and beneath are the ever-lasting arms.

—DEUTERONOMY 33:27,
DAKE'S ANNOTATED REFERENCE BIBLE

WHATEVER IT IMPLIES, THE TRUE CHRISTIAN EXPERIENCE ALWAYS INCLUDES A GENUINE ENCOUNTER WITH GOD. WITHOUT THAT THE RELIGION IS LIKE A SHADOW, A REFLECTION OF REALITY, A CHEAP COPY OF AN ORIGINAL ENJOYED AT SOME POINT BY SOMEONE WE HAVE HEARD OF.

—A.W. TOZER

CHAPTER NINE

THE PRIVILEGE OF WORSHIPING GOD

I SAIAH CHAPTER 6 is a classic text about the subject of worship. In it is written the encounter that the prophet had with God that marked his life. This event describes for us, in essence, what worship is.

> In the year that king Uzziah died I saw also the Lord sitting upon a throne, high and lifted up, and his train filled the temple. Above it stood the seraphims: each one had six wings; with twain he covered his face, and with twain he covered his feet, and with twain he did fly. And one cried unto another, and said, Holy, holy, holy, is the LORD of hosts: the whole earth is full of his glory. And the posts of the door moved at the voice of him that cried, and the

house was filled with smoke. Then said I, Woe is me! for I am undone; because I am a man of unclean lips, and I dwell in the midst of a people of unclean lips: for mine eyes have seen the King, the LORD of hosts.

—ISAIAH 6:1–5

This text contains two important truths to highlight. The first is that Isaiah has the privilege of contemplating God in His glory. The Lord removed the veil and invited His servant to gaze upon His majesty. That "unveiling" and the prophet's amazing "contemplation" are what made this encounter possible. This, in essence, is worship.

> *How do we respond correctly to a God with such dimensions of glory and character? We respond by worshiping Him in the beauty of holiness.*

Isaiah discovered that the God whom he has served was much more sublime and more powerful than he imagined. Isaiah was shaken by that vision. The glory of our Lord will always escape what the human mind can grasp, understand, and even bear.

As the Lord's anointed one, Isaiah fell to his knees and cried out when he saw his spiritual condition in the light of God's majesty. Here is the second important truth that we find here:

146

Isaiah responded to God's revelation in the best way that was humanly possible. He prostrated himself and cried out, "Woe is me! I recognize my condition, and I need you."

From the preceding we derive another especially relevant truth: before we can worship, we need God to first reveal Himself to us.

You know what? In this respect, God has always taken the first step so that you and I may be able to know Him; that's why we're here, connected through this book, because He has revealed Himself to us and we share a common faith.

Summarizing what was said above we can say:

> What is worship then? It is giving attention to God's revelation (be it a special one, the Bible, the general revelation) and to respond to it.[1]

John MacArthur, a successful Christian author, stated in an article in *Discipleship Journal* the following:

> The essence and the heart of worship is an intense desire and not selfish to give to God. That desire begins with our own surrender, then the surrender of our attitudes and our possessions, until worship becomes a lifestyle.

Allen and Borror quote William Temple, who defines worship in a profound way saying:

Worship is the awakening of the conscience of man for God's holiness. Worship is feeding the mind with the divine truth and cleaning the imagination with the beauty of God, opening the heart to God's love and surrendering the will to God's purpose.[2]

The Book of Psalms calls the entire human race to worship God in the right way:

Give unto the LORD, O ye mighty, give unto the LORD glory and strength. Give unto the LORD the glory due unto his name; worship the LORD in the beauty of holiness.

—PSALM 29:1–2

In Psalm 104:1, David tells us, "O LORD my God, thou art very great; thou art clothed with honour and majesty."

How do we respond correctly to a God with such dimensions of glory and character? We respond by worshiping Him in the beauty of holiness.

Another psalm has a series of statements and confessions of the psalmist before God that are wonderful.

In my distress I called upon the LORD, and cried unto my God: he heard my voice out of his temple, and my cry came before him, even into his ears. Then the earth shook and trembled; the foundations also of the hills moved and were shaken, because he was wroth. There went up a smoke out of his nostrils, and fire out of his mouth devoured: coals were kindled by it. He bowed the heavens also, and came down: and darkness was under his feet. And he rode upon a cherub, and did fly: yea, he did fly upon the wings of the wind. He made darkness his secret place; his pavilion round about him were dark waters and thick clouds of the skies. At the brightness that was before him his thick clouds passed, hail stones and coals of fire. The LORD also thundered in the heavens, and the Highest gave his voice; hail stones and coals of fire. Yea, he sent out his arrows, and scattered them; and he shot out lightnings, and discomfited them.

—PSALM 18:6–14

Notice the words with which this man describes God's intervention in favor of him and his children. This is not just rhetoric; it has to do with God's manifestation at a level and in a way that we are not used to seeing.

Our God is awesome! I wonder if we are adequately responding to that God who describes Himself for us in the Psalms. Do we have in mind this kind of perspective about God when we sing a psalm while we chew gum? Have we lost that sensation of awe that invaded the psalmist as well as Isaiah?

The disciples went up to the mountain with Jesus to be in God's presence, and, to their surprise, Jesus' face was

149

transformed like the brightness of the sun. His clothes were radiant with a whiteness that no soap could ever achieve (the evangelist tells us). And if that wasn't enough, while a cloud of light covered them, a voice like thunder said, "This is my beloved Son, in whom I am well pleased" (Matt. 17:5).

What were the disciples thinking?

Perhaps they said among themselves, "We thought we were with Jesus our friend, our 'buddy.' We have hung out with Him; yesterday we even played a joke on Him. But who is this One who is with us? What kind of man is this One who walks with us? He is dressed in flesh, like us, but inside He has something we don't understand, a glory that is more sublime than all the heavens!"

> *A holy life, an honest character, and devotion are essential characteristics found in those who want to get closer to God to truly worship Him.*

The disciples melted like butter at His feet!

In the dramatic ending of Job's story, the Lord spoke to question his friends' arguments. In His eternal wisdom, the Lord confronted the limitations of man before the vastness of His power and knowledge:

Where were you when I laid the earth's foundation? Tell me, if you understand.... Who shut up the sea behind doors when it burst forth from the womb...Have you journeyed to the springs of the sea or walked in the recesses of the deep? Have the gates of death been shown to you? Have you seen the gates of the shadow of death?...What is the way to the place where the lightning is dispersed...Who cuts a channel for the torrents of rain, and a path for the thunderstorm...Can you bind the beautiful Pleiades? Can you loose the cords of Orion? Can you bring forth the constellations in their seasons or lead out the Bear with its cubs?...Who endowed the heart with wisdom or gave understanding to the mind?

> —JOB 38:4, 8, 16–17, 24–25, 31–32, 36, NIV

This holy man became speechless before the words and the revelation of God, and he repented:

Moreover the LORD answered Job, and said, Shall he that contendeth with the Almighty instruct him?...Then Job answered the LORD, and said, "Behold, I am vile...Once have I spoken; but I will not answer: yea, twice; but I will proceed no further....I have heard of thee by the hearing of the ear: but now mine eye seeth thee. Wherefore I abhor myself, and repent in dust and ashes.

> —JOB 40:1–5; 42:5–6

Who is this God who wants to reveal Himself to us? And who are those who are going to be able to worship Him?

The psalmist asked the same question and answered by saying:

> Who shall ascend into the hill of the LORD? or who shall stand in his holy place? He that hath clean hands, and a pure heart; who hath not lifted up his soul unto vanity, nor sworn deceitfully. He shall receive the blessing from the LORD, and righteousness from the God of his salvation. This is the generation of them that seek him, that seek thy face, O Jacob.
>
> —PSALM 24:3–6

A holy life, an honest character, and devotion are essential characteristics found in those who want to get closer to God to truly worship Him. Not just anyone can expect to enter His presence. In fact, the figure in the Old Testament is that of one man, dressed in holy attire who could witness the warmth of the light that illuminated the holy of holies with glory. One man, one time per year, with one sin offering. No one else!

Who then could qualify? *Nobody*, except the Perfect One who in one day and with one offering opened the way for all: Jesus the Lamb!

The veil of separation has since been rent. The privilege is now extended to all, but not all enjoy it.

WORSHIPING GOD IS NOT CHEAP...IT COSTS YOU YOUR LIFE.

CHAPTER TEN

STEALING GOD'S HEART

WHO ARE THOSE who enjoy His presence? They are the ones who desire God, and to them the secret of His presence is revealed. I call them the "privileged ones" of God. But does God have favorites? In a sense, no. But it is true that He honors with His friendship those who decide to put Him first. Let's see who are these blessed ones.

WORSHIP IS THE PRIVILEGE OF THOSE WHO ARE HUNGRY

Moses was a man who witnessed mighty works of God throughout his life. He never forgot the first time he

155

responded to the voice of the Eternal coming from the bush. From that moment, God's voice guided him in the face of a rebellious empire's challenge, and it also comforted him in the face of the unbelief of his own people. Moses had heard God's voice. How many of us could say the same?

Moses also witnessed the manifest powers of God such as fire, darkness, blood, and death, which afflicted Egypt. With each plague, God's fingerprint was recorded on the soul of this hero of the faith.

Who could forget the scene of the sea parted in two, as if opening a path to freedom for a people about to perish? Perhaps Moses never forgot the shiver he felt when the drops of salt water collided with his skin. In his mind, he remembered again and again the incandescent fire guiding them as they escaped that terrible night when Pharaoh pursued them.

Once they were delivered from the Egyptians, Moses got up and said:

> I will sing to the LORD, for he is highly exalted. The horse and its rider he has hurled into the sea.... He is my God, and I will praise him, my father's God, and I will exalt him. The LORD is a warrior; the LORD is his name.... Who among the gods is like you, O LORD? Who is like you—majestic in holiness, awesome in glory, working wonders?
>
> —EXODUS 15:1–3, 11, NIV

Who could doubt the authenticity and sincerity of these words in this song of Moses? Especially coming from a man whose very existence can only be explained by God's supernatural intervention saving him from the waters. He himself was a miracle.

And what about the shaking knees and the beating heart when the voice like a trumpet called him from the thick cloud on the mountain? The people ran away while their leader went up the mountain and into the dark clouds to listen and to see God. Moses knew God, and he had privileges that others had refused.

In Exodus 33:11–18, however, the leader of Israel reveals to us a secret of the spiritual life when he intercedes for the people.

The tablets were broken into thousands of pieces because the people had broken the covenant. In the face of such tough sin, God told Moses, "Do you know what, Moses? I have bad news for all of you. I had promised to take you to the Promised Land, but I can't go with you. If these people do something like this again, I may respond in wrath and consume them. Therefore, I am not going with you; I will send an angel."

"Lord, if I have found grace before Your eyes, then reveal to me whom You will send, because we don't want to go to a land where we won't have Your presence. We don't want a Promised Land without You," begged Moses.

"Very well, I will go with you. You have found grace before My eyes, and I have to say yes," answered the Lord.

Moses obtained the first thing; now he asks the second one: "If Your presence will not go with me, then do not send us up from here. Because how will they know that we are Your people if Your presence does not go with us?"

"I will also give you this which you ask; I will go with you and give you peace," the Lord confirmed to him.

Then Moses asks the third thing: "Show me your glory" (Exod. 33:18, NIV).

> *If the holy place of God's presence is destined for someone, it is for people like Moses who are hungry for God.*

In other words, Moses said, "I beg You that You let me see Your face; let the veil that has always been there be removed, because I want to worship You. I want to know You."

The same man who saw God, who heard His voice, is also the same man for whom it was not enough to see the works and miracles revealed to him. This man was pursuing God!

If the holy place of God's presence is destined for someone, it is for people like Moses who are hungry for God. People who are not satisfied with the experiences of the past, who are not content to just read or sing about God. That place is reserved for those who do not stop until they receive a glimpse of the glory of the God they worship. God answers immediately when He finds someone like this.

A. W. Tozer, in his book *The Pursuit of God*, said that God waits to be desired; He doesn't show His face to just anyone but only to those who are really hungry for Him.

The people of Israel also heard the voice from the mountain calling them, but when they arrived within a certain distance, they ran away when they saw the splendor and terror of that fiery mountain. But Moses crossed the line, even if in the process of searching for God he had to die. Those are the kind of people to whom God gives the privilege of worshiping Him.

Why does worshiping in the church become so frivolous and trivial? Could it be that our hearts are not really hungry for God? How do we awaken this thirst?

The theologian A. W. Tozer also said that God is always ahead of us, and before man seeks God, God seeks man. But His previous work must find in us a positive reciprocity so that we can live the experience of His presence.

It is a miracle that we want to seek God! He Himself produces such a miracle in His children. God Himself captivated Moses with miracles and wonders, and that is what He wanted to produce in His children also.

God doesn't give away miracles everywhere as if they were candy just so that you can enjoy them. He manifests His signs and miracles to seduce the hearts of His children toward Himself. God already did His part; now He is waiting for us to reciprocate with longing, seeking Him.

This is in accordance with what A. W. Tozer explains about Psalm 63:8:

> My soul clings to you; your right hand upholds me.
>
> —NIV

The Lord answered Moses and said, "You are asking something big. I can't give you exactly what you ask, but come early tomorrow morning."

The next day Moses was there, on the summit of the mountain, waiting for God to appear.

The heavens came down upon that mountain. The intensity of the glory was such that God took Moses and hid him in the cleft of a rock. Then He took away His hand so that this man could see only the Lord's back. God declared His name and passed in front of Moses in all His glory, saying, "The LORD, the LORD, the compassionate and gracious God, slow to anger, abounding in love and faithfulness" (Exod. 34:6, NIV).

This was the first time God manifested this meaning of His name, and Moses was the first to hear it.

Immediately, Moses prostrated himself to worship, and sometime after that when he came down from the mountain, his face manifested the glory he had witnessed before God for several days. That glory had transformed him because he was hungry and thirsty for God. He didn't have any commitments with anyone, not even with the experiences and the glories of the past. He was thirsty for God.

WORSHIP IS THE PRIVILEGE OF THOSE WHO BELIEVE

Every time God approached Abraham, He did it to offer something to him. The first time He had an encounter with him, He said, "Go out from this land where you are, and I will make you great and will bless you." (See Genesis 12:1–3.) The second, third, and fourth time they encountered each other at different times in this man's life, the Lord always said to him, "Look at the stars, and see if you can count them; that's how your offspring will be. Look at this valley in front of you, look at the land before you, do you think you can measure it? That's the land I have given you."

Abraham had grown accustomed to those promises of God he received with each encounter he had with Him. It was like a child whose first question as he welcomes his dad back from a trip is not, "How did it go, Dad?" Instead he asks, "What did you bring me?"

That night Abraham saw the Lord approach his tent and got so excited that instead of waiting for the Lord "to ring the bell," he went out to meet Him and said, "Lord, um…how are You?"

"Come, Abraham. I don't have anything to offer you this time," said the Lord.

"It doesn't matter, Lord; we're friends. After so many years, You don't have to bring me a present every time You come from a trip! What do You need?"

"What do I need?" asked the Lord.

"Yes."

"I have come to ask you something. I have come to ask you…"

"Yes? What do You wish to ask?"

"I have come to ask you for the sign of the covenant. I have come to ask you for that which you care for so deeply. I come to ask you for that which has stolen your heart, that which compelled you to keep a journal now that you are an old man. I have come to ask you for that which made your heart beat faster. I have come to ask you for your dreams, for what you love the most."

The Lord silently turned aside. Abraham looked to the ground and walked back to his tent, also in silence.

Very early the next day, he packed his things, kissed his wife on the forehead, and when she woke up, he said to her,

"My love, we're going on a trip."

"What? Where?" she asked, surprised.

"Don't worry; the Lord asked me to worship Him. He gave me the privilege to worship Him," her husband answered.

Three days he journeys, asking himself, "What's going to happen? What am I going to do? How, after so many years? How can He ask this if He knows it is breaking my heart? How, if He is my friend, is He asking me to do something that causes me so much pain?"

At the end of the three days, the mountain is close by, and the Lord says to him, "This is the mountain. You know what you have to do."

Abraham leaves his servants nearby and says to them, "Don't worry; we're going up the mountain to worship. We'll be back."

That mountain seems to take an eternity to climb, each step getting heavier, as he goes up with a heart that trusts.

His son, restless, looking around, begins to go over things. He checks that the knife is in the pocket, the ropes, the matches, the kerosene. Everything is ready. Then he asks Abraham, "Hey, Daddy, I see everything is ready to worship the Lord, but I can't find the offering."

Abraham, evasive, says to him, "Don't worry, my son. Since God called us to worship Him, He will provide the lamb."

When they get to the top, they build the altar. When his son finishes placing the firewood, he takes the boy's hands and ties them behind his back. The boy begins to yell, "Dad, what are you doing?"

He picks him up, places him on the firewood, brings a piece of cloth, and covers his eyes. The boy continues to yell, "Dad, have you gone crazy? What are you doing?"

His father can't say anything; he just thinks, *You don't understand, Isaac! You don't understand, and neither do I!*

He gets the knife from the pocket and lifts it up with all his strength, ready to pierce the heart of that boy, of his hope, and of his life.

You don't get excited because you know how the story ends, but Abraham didn't know it. He didn't lift up his hand and say, "Very well, Lord, I am here. Now comes Your part. You have to call me. Remember? Abraham, Abraham!"

All he knew is that he loved God without reservation. He knew the God he worshiped deserved to be worshiped even

> *Your faith is what calls you to launch out to what looks deep, but really isn't.*

if that cost him his life. He knew that his God was good, and, because of that, He was worthy of being worshiped.

During those three days he must have gone over in his mind that, if this was necessary, God would raise the child from the dead to fulfill His word, because he worshiped a God who was trustworthy, and that's why he believed in Him.

It's easy to tell the story, but not when you are at a point in your life when you have to pierce what you love and let go of what you've held on to. It's not easy to worship God when your heart is breaking into a million pieces. There is no beautiful church music because you are alone.

The challenge is for you and nobody else. It is then you have to weigh your faith, which is what sees God when the clouds blanket the sky day after day. Your faith sees God, and it dares to walk on water, even though the storm is so intense that it looks like you're going to drown. Your faith is what calls you to launch out to what looks deep, but really isn't.

Worshiping God is not cheap. Worshiping God costs you your life. If worshiping God meant singing love songs like the ones we record on an album, then it would be child's play. But every time that you and your church verbalize your passion for God, it is taken seriously to later be tested. If you don't agree with what I just said, then you wouldn't be in agreement with the first verse of Genesis 22, which says, "God tested Abraham" (NIV).

I love art, and years ago I was able to see the painting of a great artist in the El Prado Museum in Madrid, Spain. This artist depicted Abraham from behind as a strong man, whose muscles are tense at the moment he raises the knife to pierce Isaac, who was before him. What touched me the most about that painting is the angel, much more powerful than Abraham, who grabbed him by the wrist and pushed him backwards as if to say, "If I don't grab his wrist firmly, this man will run through his son, and I can't allow that."

Contemplating that painting made me cry. I could picture God from heaven yelling at the top of His voice, "Abraham! Abraham! Don't touch the boy!"

Abraham throws away the knife and prostrates himself before God, saying, "Lord, what do I do now?"

And the Lord yells from heaven, "Abraham, now I know that you fear Me and that there is nothing you would refuse Me. Now I know that your love for Me is genuine and your faith is perfect."

Instantly, Abraham hears the noise of an animal trapped among the bushes. Abraham unties the blindfold from his son's eyes and wipes away his tears. Happily, he takes that animal and sacrifices it before God.

There was great joy in heaven. The angels elbowed each other because they saw God happier than ever. An angel who had arrived late asked curiously, "Why is the Lord so happy?"

The next time Mary is mentioned is at this point. There is a party, a lot of protocol, and people celebrating Jesus. Dishes came and went, music, men eating, women cooking and looking through the windows and screens. They couldn't go in even if they wanted Jesus close. Men would look at them only to get another dish. Mary moved the screen that separated the men from the women. She was hiding something in her dress, and she approached Jesus, eyes gazing down, because she knew that probably all eyes were on her. Throwing herself to the ground, she let down her hair as only a street walker would do in public, and she took out a small bottle from her clothing. She broke it, and when she did, it shattered at the feet of Jesus.

Her perfume mixed with the sand, the sweat from His precious feet, and her salty tears. As Mary kissed the Master's feet in silence, the party came to a halt, the music stopped, the men were elbowing each other, and the women behind her were criticizing her, saying, "Is she nuts?" Another spiritual person said, "What a waste! What was she thinking?"

Some were saying that this bottle was the dowry her father had given her when she was a child to put on her body the day she would marry, or in the event that she never had that joy, someone would prepare her body as a last offering before her burial.

Whatever the case, that perfume signified a lot for that woman, but even more significant was her boldness to crash a party that she wasn't invited to and to do what was inappropriate—to prostrate herself at the Lord's feet.

When Jesus saw those men wanting to criticize her, He turned to the woman and silenced the voices of criticism saying, "Be quiet! Nobody criticize her. This woman knows who I am. She has done this for my burial. She gave me the ultimate offering that anyone could have given Me."

> *Some of us could have entire orchestras playing before us, and they wouldn't move us one inch, much less our soul, because it is not sublime music that we need; it is passion we are lacking.*

The other occasion that a woman had a similar audacity, Jesus said, "Wherever the gospel is preached, I charge you to tell what this woman has done, for her remembrance."

God loves those who are passionate for Him. You can't worship God if you don't have a heart burning with passion for Him. The church doesn't need better songs to worship, better singers, or more experienced musicians. Some of us could have entire orchestras playing before us, and they wouldn't move us one inch, much less our soul, because it is not sublime music that we need; it is passion we are lacking.

When passionate people worship, a simple guitar or the silence of a mountain is enough. Those who are passionate are not stopped by the chains that hurt the wrists or the feet. Nor does the whip on their backs rob them of their song.

The fire makes passionate people sing until they have no more breath, and they are not ashamed of dying naked before a nation.

Passionate people are the ones who have the privilege of worshiping God.

The holy, sublime, and fearful God allows Himself to be touched by those who have a passion for Him, by those who believe intensely in His goodness, and by those who are hungry for His presence. Those three things steal God's heart.

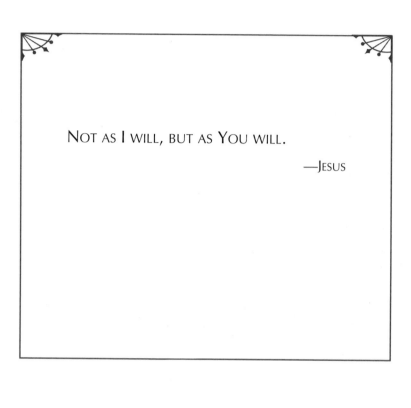

NOT AS I WILL, BUT AS YOU WILL.

—JESUS

THE GARDEN OF BROKENNESS

THE CRICKETS SANG their serenade while the amber lights began to light up in the city faraway. The place was familiar to Him. He used to spend entire nights in that stillness, and while He enjoyed the smell of the old olive trees, his soul smelled the fragrance of the Father's tender presence.

It had been a garden of refuge, but that night, His only shelter would be in prayer. That anticipated, prophetic, inescapable night. His friends were snoring, His soul was trembling, and His companion was loneliness. His prayer became anguish, so much that amidst yelling and sobbing, His forehead became drenched in sweat and blood.

Trembling as He cried, He hit the rock on which He leaned to pray, and in a loud voice He shouted to heaven, "Father, if it is possible, if there is any way, pass this cup from Me."

The human dilemma screamed from the heart of the God-man. Moses' battle occurred when he returned to Egypt, Gideon's fear before the angel's challenge was his dilemma, Jacob fought with his God at Peniel, Elijah laid under the juniper wishing to die, and Jonah cried trapped in a fish. Jonah cried because of his disobedience, but Jesus cried out because of His obedience to be confined to a mortal body.

The accelerated pulse in the earth, the angels standing in heaven, the saints from the past waiting expectantly, the future hanging by a thread—and Jesus was fighting.

What made Him shake so much? What would be the terrible thing that intimidated the brave Carpenter?

It wasn't the horror of the nails that would pierce His wrists and feet. It wasn't the thought of the pain from the ungrateful blows that would disfigure His face. He wasn't crying because of the thorns that would penetrate His forehead or the cruelty of the Roman whip that would score His back. It wasn't the pain of being sold by a friend that moved Him or the shame of dying naked before His beloved ones.

What frightened Him was the unknown—yes, the only

thing that the "All-Knowing" didn't know, what the Beloved had never suffered. The next day while He would try to painfully support Himself on His pierced feet and between the asphyxiation and the muscle cramps, He yelled, "Father, Father, why have You forsaken Me?" The last thing His eyes would see would be God's back turned away from Him in judgment instead of the eternal embrace of the Father. The Father's rejection was death itself.

A touch on the shoulder awoke Him from the nightmare. Jesus wiped the blood and sweat from His eyes to see who was there, and when He lifted up His face, the visitor hurried to retrieve his warm hand from the cold shoulder of the Master, and trembling he said, "I am sorry, my Lord."

"Who are you?" asked Jesus.

"You called me Grace, Lord," answered the messenger timidly while looking down to the ground.

The angel then came close to the Lord's ear and with a firm, but respectful, voice said, "I humbly wish to remind You, Holy Lamb, that only You are capable of doing this. If You say no, the human beings won't have hope. None of them will come back home."

His face shone with glory. Suddenly, the Lamb saw what His soul came to seek. He saw you, He saw me along with millions worshiping the Father forever.

It was then that the Lord stood up and, with His right hand

lifted, said, "Not My will, but Your will."

His voice traveled faster than the speed of light and lit up the heavens with praises, and hell was filled with fear. The angels applauded. A smile appeared on the Father's face, and a tear rolled down His cheek.

NOTES

CHAPTER 3
THE CROSSROADS OF CHANGE

1. Brennan Manning, *Abba's Child* (Colorado Springs, CO: NavPress, 1994), 40.

CHAPTER 4
GRACE IS AN EMBRACE

1. "Grace By Which I Stand" by Keith Green. Copyright © 1980 Birdwing Music (admin. by EMI Christian Music Publishing)/(admin. by BMG Music Publishing); BMG Songs, Inc. (admin. by EMI Christian Music Publishing)/(admin. by BMG Music Publishing). All rights reserved. Used by permission.

CHAPTER 6
THE MARK OF GOD

1. Arthur Burt, *Surrender* (Lake Mary, FL: Charisma House, 1997), 75.

2. "Magnificent Defeat" by Wes King. Copyright © 1997 Sparrow Song (a div. of EMI Christian Music Publishing) and Uncle Ivan Music (admin. by EMI Christian Music Publishing). All rights reserved. Used by permission.

3. Manning, *Abba's Child*, 17.

CHAPTER 9
THE PRIVILEGE OF WORSHIPING GOD

1. Ronald Allen and Gordon Borror, *Worship: Rediscovering the Missing Jewel* (Portland, OR: Multnomah Press, 1982).

2. Ibid.

NOTES

NOTES

NOTES

NOTES

NOTES

NOTES

NOTES

Resources to draw close to Him!

You will be inspired with the writings and music of Danilo Montero, a pioneer of praise and worship in Latin America. Montero, who has been called the "Spanish Max Lucado," will help you to discover a genuine relationship with the Lord.

Experience intimacy with God!

Respected worship leader and ordained minister Danilo Montero will help you to be honest with yourself and God in *El abrazo del Padre* (*The Father's Embrace*). A Gold Medallion finalist and international bestseller, this book will enable you to admit your fears, pride, and religiosity, while encountering God face-to-face. $9.99/0-88419-715-8
(Paperback)

He is your fortress!

Inspired by Psalm 27, *Fortaleza* (*Fortress*) captures Danilo Montero's passion for the presence of God. Recorded live, this Spanish album features Jeff Pitzer, Paul Wilbur, Ken Love, Jars of Clay, Delirious, Fernando Solares, Lisa Bevil, Carman, Amy Grant, and the Symphonic Orchestra of Costa Rica. *Fortaleza* will inspire you to seek the Lord.
$14.99/824477777829 (CD)
$9.98/824477777843(CS)

Walk in His steps!

Danilo Montero's *Sigueme* (*Follow Me*) will challenge you to follow in God's steps. The Spanish album's ten songs were produced by Jeff Deyo, of SonicFlood fame, and Fernando Solares, accomplished songwriter and producer.
$14.98/824477777728 (CD)
$9.98/824477777742(CS)

4334

For more information on our Spanish bestsellers, call 407-333-7177 or visit www.casacreacion.com.

Strang Communications, the publisher of both Charisma House and *Charisma* magazine, wants to give you 3 FREE ISSUES of our award-winning magazine.

Since its inception in 1975, *Charisma* magazine has helped thousands of Christians stay connected with what God is doing worldwide.

Within its pages you will discover in-depth reports and the latest news from a Christian perspective, biblical health tips, global events in the body of Christ, personality profiles, and so much more. Join the family of *Charisma* readers who enjoy feeding their spirit each month with miracle-filled testimonies and inspiring articles that bring clarity, provoke prayer, and demand answers.

To claim your **3 free issues** of *Charisma,* send your name and address to: Charisma 3 Free Issue Offer, 600 Rinehart Road, Lake Mary, FL 32746. Or you may call 1-800-829-3346 and ask for Offer # 93FREE. This offer is only valid in the USA.

---

www.charismamag.com